J. WESTON
WALCH
PUBLISHER
Portland, Maine

top SHELF
FORENSICS

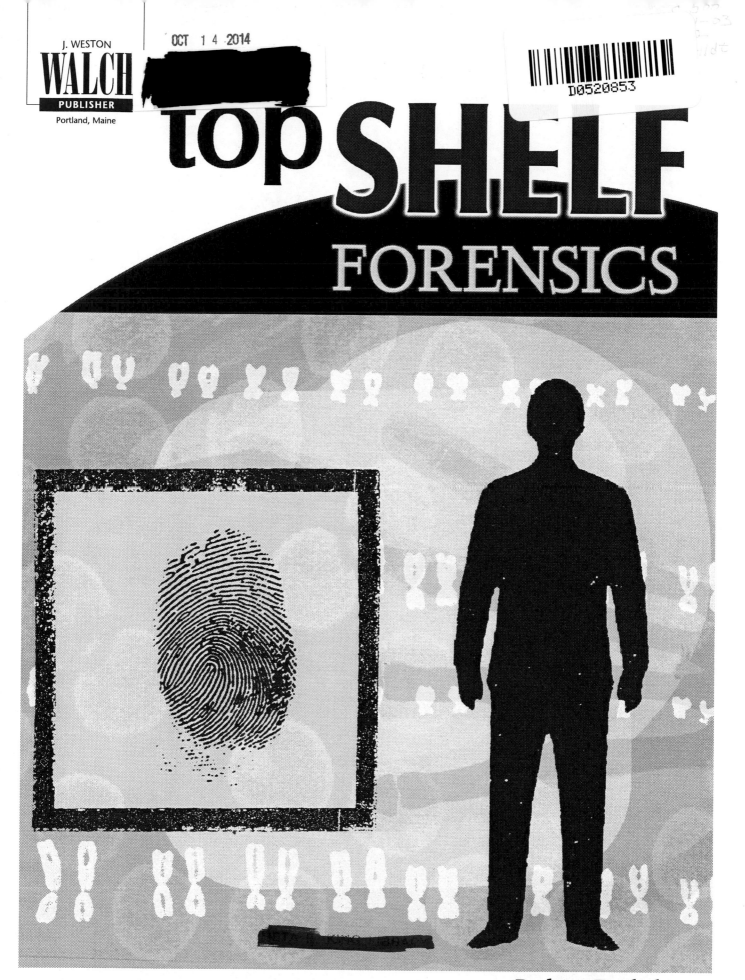

Barbara Deslich
John Funkhouser

User's Guide
to
Walch Reproducible Books

Purchasers of this book are granted the right to reproduce all pages.

This permission is limited to a single teacher, for classroom use only.

Any questions regarding this policy or requests to purchase further reproduction rights should be addressed to

Permissions Editor
J. Weston Walch, Publisher
321 Valley Street • P.O. Box 658
Portland, Maine 04104-0658

We gratefully acknowledge the support of Michigan State University's Outreach Office, Department of Chemistry, School of Criminal Justice (Forensic Science Program), and the Everett High School Administration.

1   2   3   4   5   6   7   8   9   10

ISBN 0-8251-4627-5

Copyright © 2003
J. Weston Walch, Publisher
P.O. Box 658 • Portland, Maine 04104-0658
walch.com

Printed in the United States of America

Contents

PREFACE

Introduction . . . . *vi*

National Science Standards for High School . . . . *vii*

Safety and Ethical Issues . . . . *viii*

Parent/Teacher/Student Guide . . . . *ix*

FORENSICS BACKGROUND

What Is Forensic Science? 1

The Legal System 2

TYPES OF EVIDENCE

Evidence 4

Forensic Activity: Robbery 11

Probability and Statistics 12

HAIR EVIDENCE

Hair as Forensic Evidence 15

The Morphology of Human Hair 17

Student Lab: Microscopic Examination of Human Hair 19

Student Lab: Comparison of Animal and Human Hair 25

Forensic Activity: Dognapping 27

FIBER EVIDENCE

Fibers as Forensic Evidence 31

Student Lab: Microscopic Examination of Fibers 33

Polymers 36

Student Lab: Burning Tests 37

Student Lab: Thermal Decomposition 39

Student Lab: Chemical Tests 41

Density and Refractive Index of Fibers 43

Student Lab: Examination of Fiber Cross Sections 45

Student Lab: Observing Fluorescence in Fibers 47

Student Lab: Dyeing Different Fabrics 48

Student Lab: Chromatography of Dyes 50

Forensic Activity: Attempted Abduction 53

BLOOD EVIDENCE

Blood as Forensic Evidence 56

Student Lab: Detection of Blood 60

Student Lab: Testing Human or Animal Blood 62

Forensic Activity: Assault 63

Blood Spatter Analysis 67

Student Lab: Blood Pattern Analysis 68

GLASS EVIDENCE

Glass as Forensic Evidence 69

Student Lab: Examination of Glass Pieces 71

Student Lab: Measuring the Density of a Glass Fragment 73

Refractive Index 75

Student Lab: Determining Refractive Index 76

Student Lab: Refractive Index of Glass Fragments 78

Forensic Activity: Burglary 80

Fracture Patterns 83

Student Lab: Analysis of Glass Fracture Patterns 86

SOIL EVIDENCE

Soil as Forensic Evidence 87

Student Lab: Examination of Soil 89

Student Lab: Physical Properties of Soil 90

Student Lab: Texture of Soil 92

Student Lab: Density Profile 93

Student Lab: Chemical Properties of Soil 94

Forensic Activity: Theft 96

APPENDIX I

Teaching Notes and Answer Key 99

Rubrics: Assessing Laboratory Reports 121

Rubrics: Assessing Crime Reports 122

Rubrics: Assessing Essays 123

APPENDIX II

Resources 124

Scientific Supply Companies 128

APPENDIX III

Time Line of Forensic Science 129

APPENDIX IV

Overheads, Labels, and Forms 131

Sine Table 135

GLOSSARY 137

INDEX 141

Introduction

The unprecedented interest in forensic science among students and teachers shows that it can be employed as an effective mechanism for teaching science to today's students. The advantages of this approach are:

- Forensic science is multidisciplinary. It embodies concepts in many areas, including chemistry, zoology, anatomy, genetics, physics, medicine, math and statistics, sociology, psychology, communications, and law. There is a great emphasis today on the wisdom of teaching science in a multidisciplinary fashion, and forensic science is among the best examples of this.

- Forensic science is a tool that uses the methods of science to help solve crimes by determining who committed them and how. It is also used to help with noncriminal activities, such as structural failures and mass disasters.

- Forensic science appeals to the detective in people. It can be fun to learn and use.

This text offers program materials for an introductory course in forensic science. Its primary focus is on the practice of forensic science and the analysis of physical evidence found at crime scenes. The fundamental objective is to teach the basic processes and principles of scientific thinking to enable them to be applied to problem solving in science and across all disciplines.

Forensic science presents itself as a natural vehicle for students to practice science as inquiry. For every piece of physical evidence brought

The Scientific Method
1. observation
2. inductive reasoning
3. hypothesis
4. deductive reasoning
5. theory

in for analysis, the student must apply the scientific method. The five steps of the scientific method are observation; collection and classification of data and looking for relationships; forming a hypothesis; testing the hypothesis; and developing a conclusion or opinion. Students must then be prepared to defend their conclusions based on their own empirical evidence.

The ultimate goal of this book is for students to gain confidence in their ability to make sense of complex problems that involve numerical data, evidence, logical reasoning, and uncertainty.

vi

National Science Standards for High School

The goals for school science that underlie the National Science Education Standards are to educate students who are able to

- experience the richness and excitement of knowing about and understanding the natural world;

- use appropriate scientific processes and principles in making personal decisions;

- engage intelligently in public discourse and debate about matters of scientific and technological concern; and

- increase their economic productivity in their careers by using knowledge, understanding, and skills they have acquired as scientifically literate individuals.

These goals define a scientifically literate society. The standards for content define what the scientifically literate person should know, understand, and be able to do after 13 years of school science. Laboratory science is an important part of high-school science, and to that end, we have included several labs in each volume of *Top Shelf Science*.

The four years of high-school science are typically devoted to earth and space science in ninth grade, biology in tenth grade, chemistry in eleventh grade, and physics in twelfth grade. Students between grades 9 and 12 are expected to learn about modeling, evidence, organization, and measurement, and to achieve an understanding of the history of science. They should also accumulate information about scientific inquiry, especially through laboratory activity.

Our series, *Top Shelf Science,* addresses not only the national standards, but also the underlying concepts that must be understood before the national standards issues can be fully explored. National standards are addressed in specific tests for college-bound students, such as the SAT II, the ACT, and the CLEP. We hope that you will find the readings and activities useful as general information as well as in preparation for higher-level coursework and testing. For additional books in the *Top Shelf Science* series, visit our web site at walch.com.

Safety and Ethical Issues

The *Top Shelf Science* series contains several laboratory experiments. Special care must be taken to ensure student safety when these experiments are performed. Experiments involving living organisms should be done carefully, and the health of the living specimen should be kept in mind. Here are some guidelines for general safety issues in a laboratory setting:

- Wear proper safety equipment at all times. This includes an apron, a smock, or a lab coat; safety goggles; and gloves. Do not wear open-toed shoes, such as sandals, during lab experiments.

- Do not eat or drink anything in the lab.

- Be sure to turn off heat sources when not in use.

- Perform any chemical experiments involving gas emissions within a chemical fume hood or in a well-ventilated room.

- Before disposing of chemical ingredients, be certain that they are neutralized; then dispose of them in proper containers.

- Establish a location for the disposal of sharp objects, such as broken glass or nails.

- Use extreme caution when heating solutions.

- Animals, plants, and other life forms deserve respect. Treat living specimens with care and, when possible, release them or replant them outdoors.

- Use care when using electrical appliances of any sort. Know how to recognize a short circuit or a blown fuse.

- Keep fire extinguishers on hand and properly charged, and know how to use them. Be sure that you have an ABC-rated extinguisher, as well as a Halon™ extinguisher for electrical fires.

- Follow all local, state, and federal safety procedures.

- Have evacuation plans clearly posted, planned, and actually tested.

- Label all containers and use original containers. Dispose of chemicals that are outdated.

- Be especially aware of the need to dispose of hazardous materials safely. Some chemistry experiments create by-products that are harmful to the environment.

- Take appropriate precautions when working with electricity. Make sure hands are dry and clean, and never touch live wires, even if connected only to a battery. Never test a battery by mouth.

- When using lasers, never look directly into the beam, and make sure students are conversant with the dangers of laser light.

Safety precautions unique to a given laboratory will be provided within the lab write-up itself. These safety precautions are provided as a guide only. They may be incomplete. Use common sense when working with any chemicals, electricity, or living organisms.

Parent/Teacher/Student Guide

Dear Parents, Teachers, and Students,

Thank you for choosing the *Top Shelf Science* series to help you better understand some of the difficult ideas in high-school science. We are confident that our books will help students who have a greater knowledge of the subject matter being studied; they can also be used to provide a lab-based program for students learning at home.

Each volume of the *Top Shelf Science* series is designed for a particular course of study. Within each volume, concepts build sequentially, and it is recommended that students begin with the first section and move forward.

Each book has sections that are thematically designed. The laboratory exercises associated with each section are specific to a deeper understanding of the overlying concept. In Appendix I, you will find a list of materials that are necessary to conduct each lab and Forensic Activity. Occasionally the list of materials appears with the lab or activity. A list of science equipment dealers is also provided.

In Appendix I, you will also find answers to the activities in each unit, as well as a suggested grading rubric for essays and lab reports. Share these rubrics with students so that they can correct areas that need to be corrected before the next assignment. In keeping with the national science standards, we have also included a time line of the history of each discipline. Each volume also contains an index and a glossary.

Whether you are using our product as the basis for a home school experience, a new and fresh way of supporting textbook material, or as preparation for a college placement test, we are confident that *Top Shelf Science* can meet your needs.

Thank you!

The authors and editors of *Top Shelf Science*

 **BACKGROUND**

What Is Forensic Science?

Forensic science is the study and application of science to legal matters. "Forensic" is derived from the Latin *forensis,* meaning a public forum where, in Roman times, senators and others debated and held judicial proceedings. Forensic science and **criminalistics** can be used interchangeably and cover a multitude of disciplines. The first seven subjects in the list below are those most commonly applied in crime laboratories.

> **"Forensic" is derived from the Latin *forensis,* meaning a public forum where, in Roman times, senators and others debated and held judicial proceedings.**

chemistry	anthropology
biology	psychiatry
firearms	**odontology**
document examination	engineering
photography	computer technology
toxicology and drug analysis	geology
fingerprints	environmental science
polygraphy	**entomology**
pathology	physics

A forensic scientist primarily studies the different types of evidence recovered from a crime scene. The forensic scientist must be prepared to testify as an expert witness at a trial or hearing. As such, he or she presents data, evaluates evidence, and renders an impartial opinion to the court. A forensic scientist will also perform scientific research and train others in the area of forensic science.

The Legal System

There are several different types of laws in the U.S. criminal justice system.

Statutory law is written or codified law, the "law on the books" as enacted by a governmental body or agency having the power to make laws (Congress). Statutory law is based on the Constitution, and precedents are set in appellate courts (also known as case law). The principle of recognizing previous decisions as precedents is called *stare decisis*. This allows for predictability in the law.

Civil law deals with relationships between individuals (property, contracts). It provides a formal means for regulating noncriminal relationships between individuals, businesses, agencies of government, and other organizations. Contracts, marriage, divorce, wills, property transfers, negligence, and the manufacture of products with hidden hazards are all civil concerns. It is up to the individual to bring the suit to court. Civil law is more concerned with assigning blame, as opposed to establishing intent. In civil cases, a "preponderance of evidence" is required to convict. Violations of civil law are generally punishable by fines.

> **Criminal law deals with offenses against an individual that are deemed offensive to society.**

Criminal law deals with offenses against an individual that are deemed offensive to society, causing the state to act as the plaintiff (e.g., *State of Michigan v. Smith*) by bringing charges against the accused. The roots of our law are in England, where offenders violated the King's Peace, which was considered an offense not just against an individual but against the order established under the rule of the monarch. A misdemeanor is a minor crime, such as theft, minor assault and battery, or possession of small amounts of certain illegal drugs. A felony is a major crime, such as murder, rape, armed robbery, serious assaults, dealing illegal drugs, fraud, auto theft, or forgery. In criminal cases, "beyond a reasonable doubt" is required to convict. Violations of criminal law are punishable by fines, incarceration, community service, and in extreme cases, life in prison or capital punishment (death).

Equity law is remedial or preventative (injunction, restraining order).

Public law is the regulation and enforcement of rights.

Administrative law is the law dictated by the Internal Revenue Service (IRS), Social Security Administration, military, and health care industry.

What Are the Steps in Pursuing Justice?

Once a crime is committed, it must then be discovered. The police investigate what may have happened by collecting information involved in the crime. The crime scene is documented and searched for evidence. All information gathered is assembled into a report for the prosecutor in which a suspect is named. Based on this report, the prosecutor determines if there is enough evidence to establish **probable cause**, and an arrest warrant is issued. A warrant is not required if the crime is committed in front of an officer or if the officer has probable cause that a crime has been committed (or is about to be committed). Approximately 95% of arrests occur without a warrant.

During an arrest, a suspect is read his **Miranda rights**, which include the right to remain silent and to have an attorney present. After arrest, the suspect is "booked," fingerprinted, and photographed. In this country, a person is presumed innocent until proven guilty beyond a reasonable doubt by a jury of her peers.

The suspect is taken before a court for a preliminary non-jury hearing within 72 hours of the arrest. The prosecution presents the case, and the accused has the right to cross-examine witnesses and produce favorable evidence. The court assures that the defendant has legal representation and understands the charge. The judge then determines if bail should be set or if the suspect must remain in custody. If the crime is a **misdemeanor**, the court may accept a plea at this time.

> ## The burden of proof in criminal cases rests entirely on the prosecution.

If the crime is a **felony**, the judge sets a preliminary hearing to decide if there is probable cause to bring the case to trial. The defendant can plead guilty, at which time a sentencing date is set by the judge. Otherwise, a trial date is arranged. The burden of proof in criminal cases rests entirely on the prosecution. Only approximately 50% of all persons arrested are eventually convicted, and of those, only about 25% are sentenced to a year or more in prison. Approximately 90% of cases are plea bargained!

 **BACKGROUND**

Evidence

What Is Evidence?

In law, evidence
can be divided
into two
general types:
direct evidence
and physical
evidence

In the law, evidence can be divided into two general types: direct and physical. **Direct evidence** is evidence in the form of a statement made under oath, such as a witness pointing to a person in court saying, "That's the guy who robbed the grocery store." This is also known as **testimonial evidence.** **Physical evidence** is any object or material that is relevant in a crime. It can be most any tangible thing, as large as an EP-3E spy plane, as small as a hair, as fleeting as an odor, or as obvious as a demolished federal building.

Edmond Locard (1877–1966), a French forensic scientist, espoused that there was always an exchange or transfer of material when two objects came into contact. The methods of detection may not be sufficiently sensitive, timely, or technologically advanced to ascertain its impact; nevertheless, a transfer takes place. This tenet is known as **Locard's principle.**

TABLE 1 Types of Common Physical Evidence	
drugs and toxic substances	fibers
paints	soil, glass
gunshot residues	blood
firearms and ammunition	body fluids
impressions (shoe prints, bite marks, etc.)	fingerprints
petroleum products	hair
alcohols (especially ethanol)	tissues
rubber material	pollen
resins, plastics	wood material
explosives residues	feathers
serial numbers	bones
documents	

> **Every contact leaves a trace.
> —Locard's principle**

Most evidence does not prove a fact and is termed **indirect evidence.** Some physical evidence, however, may be considered proof of fact, such as possessing a controlled substance, or a driver's blood–alcohol level of greater than 0.10%. **Circumstantial evidence** implies a fact or event. The greater volume of circumstantial evidence there is, the greater weight it carries. Probability and statistics come into play here.

So, What Good Is Evidence?

Physical evidence can:

- prove that a crime has been committed

- corroborate testimony

- link a suspect with a victim or with a crime scene

- establish the identity of persons associated with a crime

- allow reconstruction of events of a crime

> **Two legal decisions have largely governed the admissibility of scientific evidence: the Frye standard and the Daubert ruling.**

The **Rules of Evidence** define what evidence is acceptable (**admissible**) and how it can be used for the jury. Most of all, evidence must be relevant, meaning it must prove something (**probative**) and address the issue of the particular crime (**material**). Evidence is admissible if it is reliable and the presenter of such evidence is credible and competent. Generally, hearsay is inadmissible in criminal court because it is not reliable nor was it taken under oath and therefore does not allow for cross-examination. Hearsay is admissible in most civil suits.

The presenter of scientific evidence, the expert witness, must establish her credibility through credentials, background, and experience. Two legal decisions have largely governed the admissibility of scientific evidence: the **Frye standard** and the **Daubert ruling.**

According to the Frye standard (*Frye v. United States,* 1923), the interpretation of scientific evidence must be given by an expert witness and have gained "general acceptance" in the particular field of study. To meet the Frye standard, the court must decide if the questioned procedure, technique, and principles are generally accepted by a meaningful segment of the relevant scientific community. This case does not offer any guidance on reliability.

The Daubert ruling (*Daubert v. Merrell Dow Pharmaceutical, Inc.,* 1993) stated that the Frye standard is not an absolute prerequisite for admissibility of scientific evidence. This rule applied only to federal courts; however, states were expected to use the decision as a guideline in setting standards. The trial judge must assume responsibility for admissibility and validity of evidence presented in his court. Guidelines offered for judgment include the following:

1. The scientific theory or technique must be testable.

2. The theory or technique must be subject to peer review and publication.

3. Rate of error or potential errors must be stated.

4. The technique must follow standards.

5. Consideration must be given as to whether the theory or technique has attracted widespread acceptance within a relevant scientific community.

The Daubert ruling came about in response to a rapidly changing technological society. For new theories or techniques (such as DNA fingerprinting), unacceptable delays in admitting reliable evidence led to the decision.

Individual vs. Class Evidence

The best evidence is the type that can be **individualized** to a single, specific source, so that there is no doubt as to what the source of the evidence is. This type of evidence can place a suspect at a crime scene, associate a suspect with a victim, and sometimes even prove who committed a crime. Human characteristics that can be linked to or individualized to a particular person are fingerprints, DNA, handwriting, and voiceprints. The forensic scientist is always trying to individualize evidence so that it will have more value in the case. If this is not possible, the evidence may be found to be **consistent with** a particular source. This is called **class evidence.** Class evidence alone may not be very convincing in a crime, but if there are many different types or pieces of class evidence, the value can be considerable. Examples of class evidence are hair, fibers, soil, and glass fragments.

> **Evidence can place a suspect at a crime scene, associate a suspect with a victim, and sometimes even prove who committed a crime.**

Class evidence is associated with a group. Individual evidence is linked to a particular source.

For example, a tuft of fabric is found at a crime scene. It can be identified by chemical methods as to what type of fabric it is. Suppose it is found to be a polyester. Is this information helpful? Further examination can classify the fabric as part of a blue polyester shirt. A particular suspect may own a blue polyester shirt. But how common is this? Now suppose the fabric were ripped from the suspect's shirt in a large enough piece so that it can be matched exactly to the hole in the shirt, like a jigsaw puzzle. The piece of fabric is now uniquely associated (individualized) to the suspect's shirt.

Class evidence is associated with a group or class, like polyester or blue polyester shirts. Individual evidence can be linked to a particular source with a high degree of probability, like matching the torn fabric to the shirt. Individualization always involves a comparison.

EXPLORE Exploration Activities

Characterizing Your Shoes

1. What are some class characteristics of the shoes you are wearing today? Note shoe type, color, size, brand, and style name (if known).

2. How can you individualize your shoes using characteristics that will link them to you and no one else—regardless of whether someone else has the same type, color, size, and brand? Look for identifying characteristics, such as scuff marks and wear patterns. Use a sketch if needed.

3. How would you visualize or record the tread of your shoes where individual wear patterns, cuts, and marks are most likely to be found?

8

Matching Pieces of Paper

Cut five 1" × 1" squares of plain paper. Tear the five pieces in half, shuffle them, and examine the torn edges. A magnifying glass or stereomicroscope may be helpful.

4. Is the detailed shape of the edge unique?

5. Can you find any pair that matches that was not a pair earlier?

6. Would you consider the tear patterns individualized in your population of torn pieces of paper? Explain.

7. Would individualization be possible if a piece of paper were torn into three pieces and the center piece was destroyed?

8. What would you expect if pieces of paper were cut with scissors rather than torn? Would individualization be possible?

9. Use scissors to cut pieces that you think cannot be individualized. Do you think this is possible?

Use the stereomicroscope to see if you can individualize your cut samples.

10. Can you match the appropriate halves? What evidence did you use to do so?

11. What difficulty would you expect if pieces of cloth are cut with scissors rather than torn?

12. Would individualization still be possible? What factors would you rely upon to accomplish individualization of cut cloth?

Comparing Paper Matches

13. Obtain three matchbooks from your teacher and describe the characteristics of the match stems. Use the stereomicroscope.

Now, without watching, have your teacher remove a match from one of the books.

14. How can you identify which book the match came from? Are the results of your observations class or individual evidence, given only three matchbooks are in the sample population?

15. Suppose the sample were 500 matchbooks?

10

Forensic Activity: Robbery

A large appliance store was robbed, but no forced entry was apparent. A tab from a beverage can was found by one of the outside doors, causing investigators to assume that it may have been used to wedge the door for later access. The next day, the driver of a vehicle was pulled over for a minor traffic violation. In the car was a number of empty soft-drink cans, all with their tabs removed.

1. Can the tab found at the crime scene be associated with the tabless empties in the suspect's car? How would you go about trying to individualize the tab to the can?

2. How strong a case can you, the forensic investigator, establish?

 **BACKGROUND**

Probability and Statistics

"The probability of showers Tuesday is 80%." "The odds of the Detroit Tigers winning two consecutive baseball games is 20 to 1." "The likelihood of winning the lottery is 1 in 250,000." "The frequency of death in an auto accident is 0.000176."

We deal with probability most every day in one form or another. The law does as well: "probable cause," "probative," "probability of an accidental match," "weight of evidence," and "beyond a reasonable doubt" are all probability terms used in our legal system.

> **Evidence is used to link or associate a suspect to a crime.**

Can evidence be quantified?

Can evidence be valued numerically, like odds at a horse race? Probability (P) is the likelihood that a certain event will occur. If $P = 0$, the event will not occur; if $P = 1$, the event will occur. Probability is usually expressed as a ratio of the number of actual occurrences to the total of all possible occurrences. So, for example, the probability of someone wearing something red in your class may be 6 out of 24, or 1 out of 4. If there are 1,000 students in your school, statistically, there should be 250 wearing something red. If only one student in your class is wearing something yellow, that is 1 out of 24, then the probability of finding a student in your class wearing red *and* yellow is:

> **Probability is the likelihood that a certain event will occur.**

$$\frac{1}{4} \times \frac{1}{24} = \frac{1}{96} \text{ therefore, } P = 0.01$$

Multiplying P by the school population gives 10, the number of students one would expect to be wearing red and yellow together.

Generalizing:

$$P = \frac{1}{P_1} \times \frac{1}{P_2} \text{ etc.}$$

for **independent events**, which means that the results of one event do not affect the results of a second event.

These probabilities are gained statistically. You may find that there are more or fewer students wearing a combination of red and

Many cases have been thrown out of court because computed probability has been overestimated.

yellow. The **Rule of Large Numbers** says that the larger the population, the more likely that the actual numbers will approach those of the computed probability:

If a given outcome or event is repeated N times, then as $N \to \infty$, $P_{actual} \to P$.

We will be dealing only with independent events in this book. However, many cases have been thrown out of court or lost because the computed probability of a random match of evidence (that is the strength of the evidence) has been overestimated because the events were not independent.

Q EXPLORE **Exploration Activities**

1. Usually, evidence is used to link or associate a suspect to a crime. More often than not, the evidence is class evidence. For example, a blue fiber is found at a crime scene. Look at your classmates; how many could have transferred a blue fiber from the clothes they are wearing? How many suspects, then, are in your class?

2. Suppose the entire student body had access to the crime site. How many suspects would there be based on the statistics from your class? Is the blue fiber evidence of value?

3. Suppose that along with the blue fiber, an orange fiber was also found. Does the combination of a blue fiber and an orange fiber improve the evidentiary value? Why?

4. Does the number of characteristics of a material and/or the number of different, relevant objects found at a crime scene improve the probability of matching the evidence, albeit circumstantial, to a suspect? Why or why not?

 BACKGROUND

Hair as Forensic Evidence

What Is Hair?

Hair is a filament composed mostly of **keratin**, a tough protein **polymer** of **amino acids**. Hair is produced in a bulb-shaped pocket in the skin, called a **hair follicle**. A complete hair has a root, shaft, and tip.

Why Do We Have Hair?

Hair provided our ancient ancestors with insulation to protect them from extreme temperatures as well as from harmful sun rays. It may have even served as camouflage, as it does in many animals. These days, we have clothes and sunscreens; however, 80% of lost body heat is through the head, so a good crop of hair can act as an insulator; and also as an attraction to the opposite sex. Hair at specific places on the body has a specialized purpose; for example, hair in our nose and ears acts as a dust filter; eyebrows were meant to shield our eyes from excessive sunlight and block sweat from our forehead.

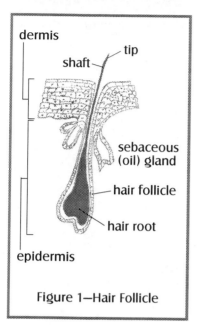

Figure 1—Hair Follicle

What Attributes of Hair Make It Useful in Forensic Science?

There are about 100,000 scalp hairs on the average person. At any one time, 80–90% are growing; the remaining are in the process of separating from the hair follicle and eventually falling out—at a rate of about 100 a day. Not only is hair common, but it is quite durable and is resistant to physical and chemical degradation. It is also persistent in that it tends to cling to things, such as fabrics. Examination of hair cannot determine sex or age. However, new laboratory techniques have enabled DNA extraction from hair under favorable circumstances. **Nuclear DNA** can be found in the hair root or adhering tissue and **mitochondrial DNA** in the hair shaft.

> **Most people lose about 100 scalp hairs a day.**

Exploration Activities

1. Describe at least one scenario in which hair could link a suspect to a victim or crime scene.

Macroscopic Observation

2. Run a comb or brush through your hair to try to capture any hairs that are no longer growing, or use the ones your teacher asked you to bring from home. Now forcibly pull out several hairs from your scalp, using tweezers if available. Arrange the hairs on a piece of white paper. List below the characteristics that can be used to describe your hair. You may wish to use a hand lens.

Save your hair samples. You will need them later.

The Morphology of Human Hair

Structure

A hair shaft is composed of three parts—the **cuticle**, the **cortex**, and the **medulla**. The cuticle is the clear, outside covering of the hair shaft. It is made up of tough overlapping scales, such as on a fish or like shingles on a roof. Humans have a much finer pattern than animals and do not show much variation.

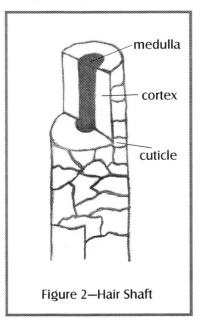

Figure 2—Hair Shaft

The cortex is made up of keratin molecules aligned parallel to the length of the shaft. Embedded within the cortex are pigment granules that give hair a lot of its color (black, brown, yellow, or red). Gray or white hair is the absence of such granules.

The medulla is a row of cells running along the center of the cortex like a canal. It may appear dark or translucent depending on the presence of air, liquid, or pigments, and it can be continuous, interrupted, or fragmented. Human hairs generally show fragmented or no medulla except for American Indians and Asians for whom the medulla is usually continuous.

Configuration

The shape of hair can also vary. It can be straight, curly, or kinky, depending on whether it is round, oval, or crescent-shaped in cross section. It is difficult to prepare a cross section of hair for microanalysis. Sometimes one can tell more about the cross section by twisting a strand back and forth on a microscope slide under low magnification. Interestingly, hair from a beard is often coarse and triangular. Particular configuration elements are statistically more common to racial origin, but there are many exceptions.

Diameter

The diameter of human hair ranges from 25 to 125 micrometers (μm). Generally, individuals have small variation within the type of hair (i.e., scalp, beard, chest, pubic, etc.).

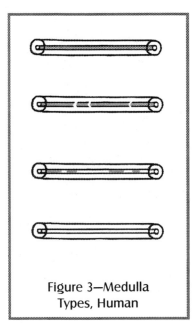

Figure 3—Medulla Types, Human

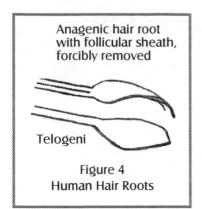

Anagenic hair root
with follicular sheath,
forcibly removed

Telogeni

Figure 4
Human Hair Roots

Root

Head hair grows at a rate of about 1 cm per month and is replaced about every 3 to 5 years with new hair. There are three stages of growth: the **anagen phase** (80–90% of hair follicles at any one time); the **catagen phase**, which is an intermediate stage; and the **telogen phase** (18–10%), in which the follicle is ready to push out the mature hair. The hairs on your brush, comb, or shoulder are telogen hairs and should reflect that in the bulbous appearance of the root with few if any pigment granules near it. Hairs that have been forcibly removed from the scalp in the anagen phase of growth may still have follicular tissue attached, may appear stretched, and may have pigment granules evident since the hair was still growing.

Tip

The tip of the hair shaft will taper to a point if it has not been cut or abused for a while. Hair that has been recently cut is squared off at the tip, but within two to three weeks it becomes rounded. Frayed hair or split ends result from dryness and lack of care (no conditioners), harsh chemicals (bleaches), or overuse of a blow dryer (too much heat).

The hair's root is embedded in the follicle, which is in equilibrium with the body's blood supply. Whatever is taken into the body is distributed into the growing hair. This is important in analyzing hair for drugs and poisons. Since hair grows at a fixed rate, a time frame of the introduction of a foreign substance can sometimes be established.

LAB

Student Lab: Microscopic Examination of Human Hair

You will be using a compound microscope to observe the structure of the hairs you have collected so far.

Materials

- Collected hair samples
- Compound microscope
- Microscope slides
- Cover glasses
- Scissors
- Mineral oil or glycerin

Procedure

1. Place the hair sample on a microscope slide and add a drop of mineral oil or glycerin (water will do in a pinch). Anchor it with a cover glass.

2. Start with the lowest magnification of the microscope, 40×. Adjust the light through the condenser for optimum viewing. Look at the entire length of your hair samples by pulling them through the liquid under the cover glass.

3. Go to 100× magnification. Draw a typical part of your hair, labeling the cuticle, medulla, and cortex. Note the degree of pigmentation in the cortex. Make your drawing at least twice as large as what you see.

4. Calculate the medullary index (MI). This is the ratio of the diameter of the medulla to the diameter of the hair. It is generally $\frac{1}{3}$ or less in humans. Estimate it if you have no means of measuring. (MI = diameter medulla/ diameter hair)

5. Twist a strand of hair back and forth on a microscope slide under low magnification. Try to tell if the cross section of hair is round, oval, or crescent-shaped.

6. The diameter of your hair can be estimated by laying a piece of wire of known diameter next to it, or comparing it to the field of view, if you know that. Some microscopes have a reticle, which is a scale in the eyepiece. Once calibrated, it can be used to measure the diameter. Or, one can use a ruled stage micrometer, which is a microscope slide with lines 0.01 or 0.001 mm apart. Measure the diameter of a strand of your hair.

7. Examine the root end of your hair samples at 40× and higher, if necessary. You should look at an anagenic root that was forcibly removed and a telogenic, mature hair root that you obtained by combing or brushing. Sketch and label the samples you observe.

8. Cut a sample of your hair with sharp scissors. Examine the tip. Compare it with the tip of one or two of your samples. Draw and label each tip. Bleached hair will appear light, even yellowish.

9. Observe a hair strand that has been dyed if one is available. The dye penetrates the cuticle and into the cortex.

10. Pluck a hair from your eyebrow, eyelash, arm, or other part of your body and compare it to your scalp hair. Draw and label the sample.

11. Examine the structure of a section of scalp hair from three other students. Draw and label a typical section from each person. You should be looking at color, medulla, diameter, and any unusual characteristics.

Conclusions

1. In step 3 in the Procedure section, are the hairs you observed the same throughout?

2. What is the value of the medullary index as found in step 4 in the Procedure section?

3. When you stretched your hair in the earlier section of the lab, was it straight, curly, or kinky? What did you observe when you twisted the hair in step 5 in the Procedure section?

4. Is the diameter of your hair constant for most of its length?

5. Is there evidence of any hair treatment in the samples you observed in step 8? How can you tell that a hair has been dyed?

6. How does the hair you observed in step 10 in the Procedure section compare to your scalp hair? How does it differ? What significance does this have?

7. How do the hairs you observed in step 11 differ from one another?

8. Fill out Table 1. In boxes 1, 2, 3, and 4 write the names of the students whose hair you studied.

TABLE 1	The Comparison of Characteristics of Human Hair				
Characteristic	**Yourself**	**1**	**2**	**3**	**4**
Color					
Length (cm)					
Medulla					
Diameter					
Configuration					
Tip					
Cosmetic Treatment					

9. What have you learned? Based on the data in the table above, can hair be used as evidence? Under what circumstances?

10. Your teacher will poll the class and tabulate the seven scalp-hair characteristics listed in Table 2 for each student. Place the number of students with that specific trait in the third column; include yourself. For example, if there are 13 blondes in your class, place the number 13 in the third column opposite blonde.

TABLE 2 Comparison of Scalp Hair Characteristics for the Entire Class		
Characteristic	Yours	Everyone
1. Color White Gray Blonde Brown Black Red No color—bald		
2. Length (cm) Under 3 cm 3–8 cm 8–15 cm 15–30 cm 30–50 cm over 50 cm		
3. Medulla Absent Fragmentary Interrupted Continuous		
4. Diameter 20–40 μm 40–60 μm 60–80 μm 80–100 μm 100–120 μm		
5. Configuration Straight Curly Kinky		
6. Tip Cut Split Frayed Rounded Pointed		
7. Cosmetic Treatment None Bleached Dyed Other		

11. Based on the data tabulated in Table 2, can hair be used as evidence? Under what circumstances? Within your class, is your hair unique? Could it be classified as individual evidence?

22

 **Exploration Activities**

Probabilities

Hair is considered class evidence in forensic science. Depending on the circumstances, its evidentiary value or importance is based on statistics. What are the chances that a hair came from a suspect or a victim? If there are only three possible suspects, a blonde, a brunette, and a redhead, and the circumstantial evidence consists of a red hair, then there is a 100% probability that the redhead committed the crime. However, if all three suspects have red hair, then the probability of choosing the perpetrator is one out of three. Not good enough! In this case, one would hope for more hair characteristics, or other circumstantial evidence. As the number of characteristics or objects linking a suspect increases, so does the probability of association or involvement.

1. A class has the following makeup:

Hair Color	Girls	Boys
Blonde	6	4
Brown	4	7
Red	0	1
Black	6	2

   a. What is the probability in this class of selecting the person who left a red hair at a crime scene? Show your work.

   b. A black hair?

   c. If all the boys and $\frac{1}{2}$ of the girls have short hair in each color category, what is the probability of finding the student who left a long brown hair?

d. If there are 630 students in the school, statistically how many boys would have black hair?

e. In class, if two blondes have a fragmented medulla and one other blond has hair longer than 20 inches, how many girls in school would you expect to have blond hair longer than 50 cm with a fragmented medulla? Does this make sense, or are the odds skewed?

2. Someone in your class has stuck a wad of bubble gum on the teacher's desk. Embedded in the top of it is a hair. Examination finds that it is brown, 5 cm long from bulb to tip, the medulla is fragmentary, the shaft is 85 μm in diameter, the tip is cut, and there is no evidence of any treatment. What is the probability that you can identify the culprit? Use the data from Table 2. Explain. (You may wish to reread the discussion on Probability and Statistics in the Forensics Background chapter.)

3. Compare the probability you determined above to the actual, **empirically** derived results from question 16 of the lab. Remember that the higher the probability of identification (or the lower the probability of finding another student with the same hair characteristics), the more likely that the hair from the bubble gum approaches being individual evidence.

4. If you consider your class as representative of your school's student body, how many students would you expect to find with the exact hair characteristics of the unscrupulous bubble-gum wadder? Show your work.

5. Why is probability important in forensic evidence?

Student Lab: Comparison of Animal and Human Hair

The first question asked in studying hair evidence is whether it is human or animal hair. It is estimated that there are 70,000,000 cats in the United States, 60,000,000 dogs, and millions of other domesticated animals. The following lab will explore how animal hairs differ from those of humans.

Materials

- Animal hairs
- Human hair
- Compound microscope
- Microscope slides
- Cover glasses

- Mineral oil or glycerin
- Alcohol
- Tissues
- Clear nail polish

Procedure

1. Use animal hair that you have collected, or obtain a sample from another student or your teacher. Place the hair sample on a microscope slide and add a drop of mineral oil or glycerin (water will do in a pinch). Anchor it with a cover glass.

2. Examine the sample. Draw and label what you observe. Be sure to note the animal involved.

3. Measure or estimate the medullary index (MI). This is the ratio of the diameter of the medulla to the diameter of the hair. Animal hairs have indices greater than $1/3$. (MI = diameter medulla/diameter hair)
   MI (human) < $1/3$
   MI (animal) > $1/3$

4. If possible, obtain slides of other animal hairs and make drawings of cat, dog, horse, deer, and two others of your choice. Don't forget to make the drawings twice as large as what you see. Measure the MI for each sample.

The cuticle of human hair is difficult to observe under a microscope because it is close-packed, transparent, and fine. Its structure can be delineated, however, by making a cast of hair.

5. Clean a strand of your hair by pulling it through a folded tissue moistened with alcohol to remove grease and oil.

6. Coat a microscope slide with clear nail polish and press your hair into it. After the polish becomes sticky but not dry, remove the hair and examine the cuticle impression at 40× or 100×. Draw a picture of what you observe.

7. The cuticles of different animal hairs can be quite varied and are generally much coarser than those of humans. Make a cast of your animal hair for comparison and draw it. Compare the drawing of the cuticle from your animal hair to those of other animals from your class.

Conclusions

1. How do animal hairs differ from the human hairs you have observed?

2. What is the value of the medullary index as found in step 3 of the Procedure section?

3. What is the value of the medullary index for each sample you observed in step 4 of the Procedure section?

4. How does the drawing of the cuticle from your animal hair compare to the drawings of others in your class?

 **SOLVE**

Forensic Activity: Dognapping

Ms. Abigail Beauceron, proud owner of the grand-prize winner at the prestigious 2003 Westminster Kennel Club Dog Show, was leaving Madison Square Garden in the late afternoon when someone came up behind her, knocked her down, bundled FuFu in a blanket, and quickly ran out the nearby exit to the parking garage. FuFu is a Black Russian Terrier with dark-gray hair.

The event was captured on a security video, but the only description obtained was that the perpetrator was wearing a dark jacket and a baseball cap. Police found a rather smelly wool blanket by an empty parking spot near the exit in question. Cursory examination by the officers showed some hair sticking to the fabric.

Early next morning, Ms. Beauceron received an unwelcome e-mail Valentine demanding $20,000 for the safe return of FuFu, with details of the exchange to be sent at a later time. The police quickly traced the message back to an Internet room maintained for patrons of the public library. At the time the e-mail was sent, library records showed that seven people had used the facility so far that day. While the library's time records were not precise, they did keep a sign-in sheet of each day's users.

The police detectives doggedly paid a visit to each suspect on the list and, brandishing a warrant, searched each residence and vehicle. They also took samples of scalp hair and any facial hair. By the end of the day, they were dog-tired, but satisfied with the information they had obtained.

The following facts about each suspect were taken from the police report:

- George Shepherd. DOB 4-13-79. White male. Ht 5-8. Wt 160 lbs. Eyes brown. Hair brown. Occupation: Assistant manager of a fast-food restaurant next to the Coliseum. Pets: One cat.

- Patricia Barbet. DOB 2-18-42. White female. Ht 5-4. Wt 110 lbs. Eyes blue. Hair white. Occupation: Real-estate broker. Pets: Three cats and a turtle.

- Helmut Weimaraner. DOB 7-2-65. White male. Ht 5-7. Wt 305 lbs. Eyes brown. Beard brown. Occupation: Accountant. Pets: None.

- William Setter. DOB 5-28-72. Black male. Ht 5-11. Wt 185 lbs. Eyes brown. Hair black. Occupation: Security guard at the Coliseum. Pets: Light-brown collie and a parrot.

- Akita Lau. DOB 8-7-70. Asian female. Ht 5-3. Wt 107 lbs. Eyes brown. Hair black. Occupation: Graphic designer. Pets: Doberman Pinscher.

- Fred Basset. DOB 8-28-61. White male. Ht 5-9. Wt 175 lbs. Eyes blue. Hair blonde. Occupation: Insurance salesman. Pet: Scottish Terrier with dark-gray hair. This dog was runner up for the last two years at the Westminster Show.

- Maurice Spaniel. DOB 9-14-78. White male. Ht 5-8. Wt 170 lbs. Eyes blue. Hair bald, no other facial hair. Occupation: Professional boxer. Pets: Irish setter with brown hair and a golden retriever with orange-brown hair.

1. Based on what you know now, do you have any thoughts on who would be your prime suspect(s)? Why?

2. Each investigative group will receive a package of evidence containing eight envelopes of hair samples. Your job is to ascertain if the evidence submitted can lead to the kidnapper. A Crime Report form must be completed independently by each investigator in each group with the realization that any one member of the group may be called as an expert witness at trial. Therefore, any conclusions must be justified and able to withstand cross-examination.

3. Can you tell what color a cat is from examination of several of its hairs?

CRIME REPORT

CASE NO. _____ DATE _____

NATURE OF CRIME _____

DATE OF OCCURENCE _____

TIME OF OCCURENCE _____

LOCATION _____

VICTIM _____

BRIEF HISTORY OF CASE:

TYPE OF EVIDENCE SUBMITTED FOR EXAMINATION _____
List each individual item: use Q for questioned (source unknown);
K for known (source established).

BRIEF DESCRIPTION OF METHODS USED:

29

CASE NO. _____

RESULTS:

CONCLUSIONS:

SIGNATURE _____ DATE _____

NAME OF INVESTIGATIVE GROUP _____

 **BACKGROUND**

Fibers as Forensic Evidence

What Is a Fiber?

A **fiber** is composed of many filaments twisted or bonded together to form a thread or yarn primarily used to manufacture fabric, carpet, paper, rope, and batting. A **filament** is a single strand of material of indefinite length, usually twisted with other filaments to make a fiber. For forensic purposes, fibers are classified as either natural (animal, vegetable, or inorganic) or artificial, also designated as synthetic.

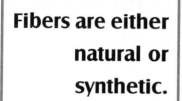

Fibers are either natural or synthetic.

Why Are Fibers Important as Forensic Evidence?

Clothing is made of fibers. Look around you—there are many types of fabric, many colors, many uses. Fibers, like hair, are easily exchanged so they can provide evidence of personal contact, and possible association between victim and suspect or object. For example, read an actual case as summarized below.

> Five-year-old Melissa Brannen disappeared from a Christmas party the evening of December 3, 1989. The suspect, Cal Hughes, left about the same time but denied having any contact with her. A search of his car found many fibers and hairs. A few black rabbit hairs found in the car could have come from Melissa's mother's dyed rabbit coat, which Melissa was fond of playing with. When she disappeared, Melissa was wearing a Sesame Street outfit of red tights, red plaid shirt, and a blue acrylic sweater, available, in limited quantities as it turned out, only from JC Penney.

> Blue fibers from the suspect's car matched the only blue acrylic fiber that could be found in Melissa's room. This provided an additional association between the victim and the suspect's car. Red cotton fibers from the car matched those from a similar Sesame Street outfit. The single blue fiber from Melissa's bedroom was found to be identical to those from a JC Penney, Sesame Street blue sweater obtained elsewhere. An experiment showed that the probability of a coincidental match of the blue fibers from the car and those from the Sesame Street outfit was extremely remote. Thus, the association of fibers linked to Melissa with those found in Cal Hughes's car allowed successful prosecution of the case. Melissa Brannen's body, however, was never found. (Summarized from Fisher pp. 115-120.)

 **Exploration Activities**

1. List some natural fibers:

2. List some synthetic fibers. (Look at the labels in your clothes, blankets, sheets, rugs, and other items for names and types. All apparel items sold in the United States must have a label listing all fibers that make up at least 5% of the fabric.)

3. List some characteristics and circumstances that could increase the odds of finding a match in the actual case described on page 31.

Student Lab: Microscopic Examination of Fibers

Fibers are considered class evidence

Fibers, like hair, are considered class evidence. They lack individuality because they are mass-produced in such large quantities. For example, in 2001 over 3.5 billion pounds of cotton yarn was produced in the United States! Some of this cotton was used to make 625 million T-shirts and tank tops, and 184 million jeans. The probability of finding a match of cotton fibers from a suspect's T-shirt and a victim seem horrendous. Any characteristics that can aid in narrowing the origin of the fiber to a limited number of sources greatly improve the value of the evidence.

Materials

- Overhead transparency sheets
- Clear 2" sticky tape
- Hand lens or stereomicroscope
- Collection of mounted fiber samples
- Mounting medium
- Compound microscope

- Microscope slides
- Cover glasses
- Mineral oil
- Collection of fabric samples
- Ruler
- Scissors

Procedure

1. Observe the collection of labeled (known) fibers provided by your teacher at 100X. Draw what you observe.

2. Place one or two fibers of each sample you were asked to bring in on an overhead transparency sheet. Carefully cover the sample with clear sticky tape, smoothing it down to remove any air pockets. Label each sample.

3. Record your observations at low magnification using a hand lens or stereomicroscope, and at 100X power. Try to identify your samples by comparing them to the known fibers. Draw a picture, if necessary, to describe your fibers.

As you learned in the Forensics Background chapter, fabric can be used as individual evidence if a swatch matches the parent cloth and fits, like a puzzle piece, exactly to the spot from which it originated. This doesn't happen very often; yet, if more than a thread or piece of **yarn** exists, the fabric itself can add to the characteristics of the evidence.

Fabric can be classified by the type of weave. The three basic patterns are shown in Figure 1:

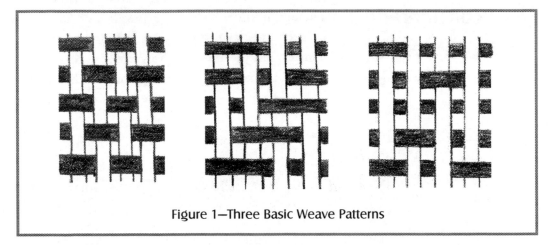

Figure 1—Three Basic Weave Patterns

4. Obtain a set of labeled fabric samples from your teacher and examine each one with a stereomicroscope. Draw the different patterns. Try to classify the different samples according to the weave and label them.

In a weave, the lengthwise yarn is called the **warp**. It is usually stronger, smoother, and more even, with a tighter twist to it than the **weft**, which is the crosswise yarn. The warp need not be the same material as the weft (this would be called a blend), nor the same color. Sometimes, the warp and the weft have different diameters in order to produce special effects, such as ribbing.

5. Measure the number of threads per inch in the warp and weft direction of your fabric samples.

6. Take a piece of 2-inch-wide clear sticky tape and press it tightly against your shirt, sweater, blouse, or whatever you are wearing above your waist. Pull it off slowly and smooth it out on an overhead transparency sheet. Observe the fibers you find.

7. Repeat this procedure with another piece of tape on your pants, skirt, or whatever you are wearing below your waist.

Conclusions

1. What properties of the known fibers did you observe in step 1?

2. What additional properties of fibers did you learn about that could increase the odds of finding a match between fiber samples?

3. Can you differentiate between warp and weft in the fabric samples you examined? Are there any blends? Note your observations on the drawings you made.

4. Are there any fibers collected in steps 6 and 7 that are *not* from the clothes you are presently wearing? Are any of the fibers the same as those you worked with in the beginning part of the lab? Explain how these fibers may have gotten on your clothes.

Polymers

How Can Fibers Be Identified by Their Chemical Properties?

All fibers are polymers, even the natural ones, as you learned in the Hair Evidence chapter. You have examined some **physical properties** of fibers. More information on identification can be gained through their different **chemical properties**, which govern their behavior in tests such as burning (oxidation), and thermal and chemical decomposition. Tables 1 and 2 describe many of the most common fibers.

TABLE 1 Common Natural Fibers			
Fiber	**Source**	**Chemical Description**	**Common Uses**
Hair	mammals	protein	apparel, blankets
Silk	insects	protein	apparel
Cotton	plant	cellulose	apparel, textiles
Linen	plant	cellulose	tablecloths, napkins
Rayon	plant	regenerated cellulose	apparel, upholstery, curtains
Acetate	plant	altered cellulose	apparel, curtains
Fiberglass	sand	silica	insulation

TABLE 2 Common Synthetic Fibers			
Fiber Type	**Chemical Description**	**Trade Name**	**Common Uses**
Acrylic	polyacrylonitrile	Creslan, Acrilan, Orlon	home furnishings, cigarette filters
Aramid	aromatic polyamide	Kevlar	protective vests, rope, sails, sporting goods
Modacrylic	acrylonitrile-vinyl, chloride copolymer	Dynel	apparel, household furnishings, stuffed toys
Nylon	polyamide	Antron, Meryl	apparel, household furnishings, rope, seat belts, tents
Olefin	polyethylene, polypropylene	Innova, Spectra	sportswear, household furnishings, rope, bags
Polyester	polyaromatic esters	Dacron, Kodel, Fortrel	apparel, household furnishings, fiberfill, auto upholstery, rope
Spandex	segmented polyurethanes	Lycra, Clearspan	stretchable apparel

 **LAB**

Student Lab: Burning Tests

How a fiber burns, its odor, and the nature of the ash or residue that results can aid in its identification. In this lab, we will observe characteristics of several identified fabrics and then use that information to identify an unknown fabric.

Materials

- Identified fabric samples
- Unknown fabric sample
- Tweezers or forceps
- Bunsen burner

Special Safety Consideration

Use caution when operating the Bunsen burner.

Procedure

1. Pull a bundle of fibers; about 1-mm thick at most, from each of the labeled fabric samples provided by your teacher. Hold the bundle with tweezers or forceps and bring it *slowly* into the open flame of a Bunsen burner or alcohol lamp. Note odor, whether the fabric supports combustion when you *slowly* remove it from the flame, the color of the flame, type of ash or residue, and the color of the smoke.

2. If you think you are dealing with a blended fabric—that is, a fabric in which the warp threads are a different generic material than the weft— unravel and separate the crosswise threads from the lengthwise ones. Twist each group into a bundle and check burning characteristics of each.

3. Fill in Table 3 using words such as scorches, smolders, fuses, melts, glows, shrinks, sizzles, flickers, flares, sputters, burns fast, burns slow, smoky, sooty, and so on. The ash or residue can be light gray, black, dark gray, shiny, clumpy, beady, sticky, feathery, and so on.

4. Include in the burn tests the unknown fabric that your teacher gave you.

37

Conclusion

1. What do you think the unknown fabric is? Why?

TABLE 3 Burn Test Results					
Fiber	Behavior Nearing Flame	Behavior in Flame	Behavior Leaving Flame	Odor	Ash or Residue
Cotton					
Linen					
Silk					
Wool					
Acetate					
Acrylic					
Nylon					
Polyester					
Rayon					
Olefin					
Fiberglass					
Unknown					

Student Lab: Thermal Decomposition

When polymeric materials are gently heated, they often decompose to their monomer building blocks or other simple characteristic products. For example, acetate fibers decompose to form acetic acid which turns blue litmus paper red.

Materials

- •Identified fabric samples

- •Unknown fabric sample

- •Bunsen burner

- •Red and blue litmus paper

- •Lead acetate solution

- •Filter paper

- •Test tubes

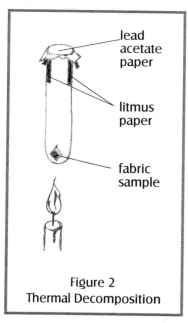

Figure 2
Thermal Decomposition

Special Safety Consideration

Use caution when operating the Bunsen burner.

Procedure

1. Place less than $\frac{1}{2}$-centimeter-square piece of known fabric or a bundle of fibers in the bottom of a 13-mm test tube.

2. Wet a piece each of red and blue litmus paper and stick both to the inside of the neck of the tube. The strips must not touch each other. Cover the top of the test tube with filter paper cut to size, then moisten it with a drop of lead acetate solution.

3. *Gently* heat the base of the test tube. Observe what happens to the lead acetate paper, the red litmus paper, and the blue litmus paper. Observe any residue. Record all your observations in Table 4.

4. Repeat the procedure for all fabric samples provided to you. Include in the thermal decomposition tests the unknown that your teacher gave you.

Conclusions

1. Why do silk and wool decomposition products turn lead acetate paper brown or black? Show the chemical equation.

2. What do you think the unknown fabric is? Why?

TABLE 4 Thermal Decomposition Test Results					
Fiber	Lead Acetate	Red Litmus	Blue Litmus	Residue	Other
Cotton					
Linen					
Silk					
Wool					
Acetate					
Acrylic					
Nylon					
Polyester					
Rayon					
Olefin					
Fiberglass					
Unknown					

 **LAB**

Student Lab: Chemical Tests

The chemical composition of a polymer determines its chemical properties as well as many of its physical properties. These tests will look into solubility and chemical reactions of different fabrics in an effort to classify and identify them.

Special Safety Considerations

The chemicals you will be using in this activity involve strong acids, bases, and solvents, all of which can irritate the skin, cause irreparable damage to your eyes if not immediately washed, and dissolve your clothing, as you will see. Wear safety glasses, gloves, and an apron. Clean up spills, even a drop, at once. Report any accidents to your teacher. Wash your hands after the lab.

Materials

- Identified fabric samples
- Unknown fabric sample
- Hand lens or stereomicroscope
- Acetone
- Bleach

- Sodium hydroxide (NaOH)
- Hydrochloric acid (HCl)
- Sulfuric acid (H_2SO_4)
- 24-well plates
- Stirring rods or toothpicks

Procedure

1. For each test, use only a few short fibers from the different fabrics provided by your teacher. If you think you are dealing with a blended fabric, unravel and separate the warp threads from weft and test them both.

2. Arrange your samples in the 24-well plates so that you can test each one in each of the five reagents: acetone, bleach, 6M sodium hydroxide, 6M hydrochloric acid, 6M sulfuric acid.

3. Add enough reagent to cover each sample. You may use a toothpick or stirring rod to mush the fabric into the liquid. After 15 minutes, record your observations in Table 5. It may be helpful to view results with a magnifying lens or a stereomicroscope with light transmitted through the well plate.

4. Include in the chemical tests the unknown fibers that your teacher gave you.

Conclusion

1. Can you tell what the unknown fabric is on the basis of these tests alone? If not, what is the use of such testing?

TABLE 5 Chemical Test Results					
Fiber	Acetone	Bleach	NaOH	HCl	H_2SO_4
Cotton					
Linen					
Silk					
Wool					
Acetate					
Acrylic					
Nylon					
Polyester					
Rayon					
Olefin					
Fiberglass					
Unknown					

42

BACKGROUND

Density and Refractive Index of Fibers

> **The more properties observed in a fiber, the greater the probability of matching it to a source.**

What Other Physical Properties of Fibers Are Useful in Identification?

The more properties or characteristics that can be observed in an unknown fiber, the greater the probability of identification and matching it to a source; or, as forensic scientists say when referring to a known and an unknown piece of trace evidence, finding a common source.

The density of a fiber may vary with its composition; likewise its refractive index. (See the Glass Evidence chapter.) Such physical properties are especially useful for small single fibers and are non-destructive.

TABLE 6 Density and Refractive Index of Fibers		
Fiber	Density, g/cm^3	Refractive Index
Cotton	1.45–1.60	1.53, 1.58
Silk	1.20–1.28	1.54, 1.59
Wool	1.28–1.35	1.54, 1.55
Acetate	1.28–1.35	1.47
Acrylic (Orlon®)	1.1–1.2	1.51
Modacrylic (Dynel®)	1.28–1.35	1.53
Nylon	1.1–1.2	1.53, 1.54
Polyester	1.35–1.45	1.57, 1.60
Rayon	1.45–1.60	1.52, 1.54
Olefin	0.90–0.95	1.50 (pe); 1.54 (pp)
Fiberglass	2.56	1.54
Water	1.00	1.33

 **Exploration Activity**

1. Describe a simple density experiment to differentiate between a polyolefin and a polyester fiber.

Student Lab: Examination of Fiber Cross Sections

When hot or in solution, synthetic fibers (artificial and altered natural material, such as rayon, acetate, and glass) are extruded through a **spinnerette**, which is a nozzle similar to a shower head. In this way, a bunch of very long filaments can be formed very quickly. The holes in the nozzle may be different shapes; thus the cross section of fiber can be an important distinguishing feature.

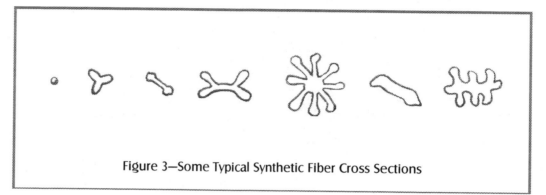

Figure 3—Some Typical Synthetic Fiber Cross Sections

The preparation of fibers for a cross-section microscopic examination is tedious, especially without expensive equipment; however, it is worth a try.

Materials

- Top of margarine container
- Duco Cement®
- Sewing needle
- Thread
- Scissors
- Acetone

- Aluminum foil
- Toothpicks
- Compound microscope
- Synthetic fibers
- Razor blade (single edge)
- Mineral oil or glycerin

Special Safety Consideration

Use caution when working with a razor blade.

Procedure

1. Cut a 1 × 2 inch piece of plastic from the top of a margarine container. Double-loop a piece of thread through a #12 sewing needle and push it all

the way through the plastic, holding on to the loose ends so they don't go through the hole. When the thread comes out of the eye of the needle, you will have a loop.

2. Tighten the loop and place a small bundle of fibers halfway into the loop. If necessary, untwist the yarn so it will unravel. Now pull the loose ends of the thread slowly through the hole until you have half the bunch of fiber on the top. Anchor the fiber with your finger and pull the thread out of the protruding bunch on the bottom of the plastic. Still anchoring it, cut the bunch of fibers close to the plastic, and repeat on the other side.

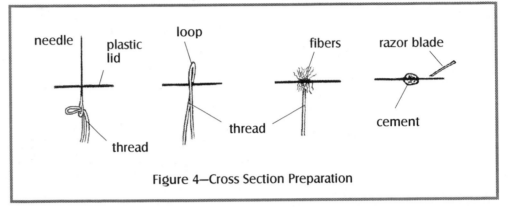

Figure 4—Cross Section Preparation

3. Dilute clear Duco Cement® about half with acetone. A small piece of aluminum foil molded into a spot plate or small, hollow depression can act as a mixing bowl. Use a toothpick to mix. Apply a small amount of the cement to each side of the bunch of fibers by swiping the toothpick across the plastic top. The idea is to get enough cement in the hole but not very much on the plastic. Allow the cement to dry (it doesn't take long when placed about an inch from an ordinary incandescent bulb).

4. Using a single-edge razor blade, cut through the dried cement with the blade almost parallel to the plastic top. Do not "saw" it. Repeat on the other side of the top.

5. Wet the area with a drop of water, mineral oil, or glycerin, and observe at 100×. Draw and label the cross section of your fiber sample.

Conclusion

1. Compare the cross section of your fiber sample with those from different samples that may have been examined. How do they differ from one another?

46

LAB   Student Lab: Observing Fluorescence in Fibers

What Is Fluorescence?

Fluorescence is the process of absorbing light of a particular wavelength (energy) and re-emitting it at a longer wavelength (lower energy). Some fibers will fluoresce when exposed to ultraviolet radiation. Fluorescence can result from the chemical and crystalline properties of the fiber itself, from dyes, or from **optical brighteners** and other agents added to the fabric. Some laundry detergents and bleaches also contain optical brighteners. Fluorescence can be diminished by washing and by wear. Nevertheless, fluorescent properties are useful for comparing fibers of a common origin as well as spotting fibers for collection.

Materials

- Fabric samples
- UV (ultraviolet) lamp

Special Safety Consideration

Ultraviolet light can damage your eyes. Do not look directly into any UV light source.

Procedure

1. Observe the set of known fabric samples provided under short-wave and long-wave ultraviolet radiation.

2. Take several fibers of the most fluorescent fabric and place them on a sleeve of a shirt or coat. Have a lab partner find them.

3. Observe various articles of clothing that people are wearing in class.

Conclusions

1. Describe the results you noted in step 1 of the Procedure section.

2. Do many of the clothing items you observed in step 3 fluoresce? Are they all the same color?

3. How does fluorescence help you identify a material?

Student Lab: Dyeing Different Fabrics

Color is very important as a matching characteristic of a fabric or fiber. Even the constituents of the dye itself can sometimes be separated and matched to an unknown.

Different types of fabric react to a dye molecule in different ways, depending on the chemical composition of the fiber, its surface treatment, the molecular makeup of the dye itself, and any subsequent chemistry it may experience. Therefore, how a fabric accepts a particular dye can be used to identify and compare samples, especially if the fabric is not dyed.

Materials

- Multifiber ribbon
- Dyes (Testfabric Stain #1 and #2)
- Identified fabric samples
- Unknown fabric sample

- Acetic acid
- 50 mL beakers
- Scissors

Procedure

1. To illustrate how different types of fabric take a dye, soak a 1-cm-wide strip of multifiber ribbon in Testfabric Stain #1. Repeat with a new strip in Testfabric Stain #2. The multifiber ribbon consists of 13 different fiber strips woven together into a single ribbon (see Figure 5). Be aware that the warp or lengthwise yarn is a synthetic if you want to examine a particular fiber type.

2. Stain about 1 square centimeter of each of your known fabric samples and compare to the ribbons. Be sure to rinse each sample thoroughly in hot tap water to set the dye; then blot it dry.

3. Test your unknown fabric and determine its identity by means of the dye test.

4. Fasten each strip of dyed ribbon and all the fabric samples on a separate sheet of paper.

Conclusions

1. What are the similarities and differences you noted? Explain any differences observed.

2. What do you think the unknown fabric is? Why?

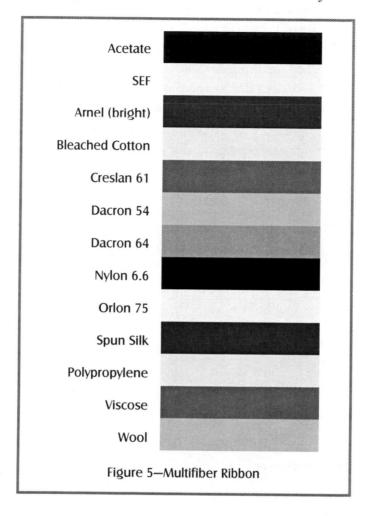

Figure 5—Multifiber Ribbon

Student Lab: Chromatography of Dyes

Dyes used to color fabric may be composed of several constituents. Indeed, there are more than 7,000 different color formulations. Sometimes these can be separated by liquid **chromatography**. Chromatography is a method of separating components of mixtures based on preferential adsorption, or partitioning of the components. In paper chromatography, the cellulose of the paper acts as the adsorbing medium. In **thin-layer chromatography (TLC)**, silica gel or alumina selectively adsorbs the components of the mixture. A **chromatogram** is the record of the separation. A chromatogram of a dye extracted from a colored fabric sample, therefore, may be compared to others to find a match. This technique is used in forensic science to distinguish inks and to analyze for drugs and poisons.

Materials

- TLC plates or chromatography paper
- Sodium hydroxide (NaOH)
- Capillary tubes (open ended)
- Hot plate
- Ruler
- Scissors
- 250 mL beakers
- Watch glasses

- Filter paper
- Blue fiber samples
- UV light
- Iodine crystals
- Ethyl acetate
- Ethanol
- n-butanol
- Acetone
- Ammonium hydroxide

Special Safety Considerations

Sodium hydroxide solution is corrosive; skin burns are possible so, wash your hands well or wear gloves. Sodium hydroxide solution is very dangerous to the eyes because it dissolves protein; wear safety glasses.

Procedure

1. The first step is to extract the dye from the fabric sample. Cut a $\frac{1}{2}$-centi-meter-square piece of colored fabric to be tested, or an equivalent wad of thread or yarn, and place in a small test tube.

2. Add 5 or 6 drops of 0.5M NaOH. Be sure the fabric is immersed. Place in a boiling water bath for 15 minutes. Record the color of the fabric and the color of the extraction solution.

3. On a 1″ × 3″ precut TLC (or 1″ × 4″ chromatography paper) strip, draw a light pencil line across the strip 1 cm above the bottom. Label the top with a sample description.

4. Using an open-ended capillary tube, spot one drop of the extracted dye solution on the center of the line. Be gentle so as not to dislodge the silica gel adsorbing medium. Keep the spot small. Repeat 10 times, allowing the drop to dry before each application. Using a hair dryer or placing the strips on a hot plate on "low" will hasten the process. The idea is to get as concentrated a spot as possible.

5. Do not be discouraged if there is no color or it is very faint. Put a drop on filter paper and check it with the UV lamp. If nothing is there, then consider another extraction reagent if available, such as a weak acid or an organic solvent like methanol.

The chromatographic developing chamber can be a large beaker lined with filter paper. Separation is hastened in the solvent atmosphere that the saturated filter paper provides.

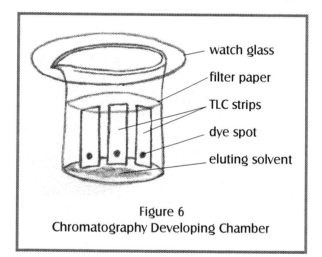

Figure 6
Chromatography Developing Chamber

Special Safety Consideration

Iodine is toxic by ingestion and inhalation. It is corrosive to the eyes and respiratory tract, and is a skin irritant. Use it in a well-ventilated area, and do not place your face close to the beaker when you remove the cover.

Procedure

1. Pour $\frac{1}{2}$ a centimeter of the developing or **eluting** solvent in the bottom of the beaker, cover with a watch glass or aluminum foil, and let it equilibrate for 15 minutes. Lean the prepared and labeled TLC strips against the filter paper, spot side down. The solvent level should be well below the dye spot. Replace the cover. When the solvent front is within 1 or 2 cm of the

top, remove the chromatogram and make a mark at the solvent front before it evaporates (see Figure 7). Lay the strip out on a paper towel to dry.

2. Sometimes invisible spots can be developed by immersing the chromatogram in iodine vapor. Place a few iodine crystals in a suitable-size beaker, prop the chromatograms against the walls, and cover with a watch glass. It won't take long, but the developed spots won't last long, as the iodine readily **sublimes**. Trace the spots before this happens.

3. Draw each chromatogram (see below), labeling each spot. Observe also under short-wave and long-wave ultraviolet radiation. Record your observations. Compare the chromatograms of the different samples. Note that your observations from the dye extraction can also be useful in distinguishing samples. Even no results (i.e., no extraction of the dye) is an important characteristic of a sample.

A chromatogram can be quantitatively described by calculating the **retention factor (RF)** for each separated component. RF is simply the distance from the original spot to the center of the separated component of the dye divided by the distance from the original spot to the solvent front. If the color and RF for a spot are the same from different samples of fabric, there is a good chance that it is the same component if experimental conditions are the same.

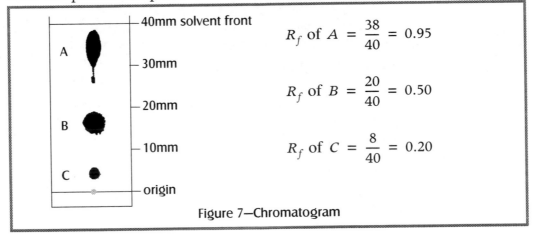

$$R_f \text{ of } A = \frac{38}{40} = 0.95$$

$$R_f \text{ of } B = \frac{20}{40} = 0.50$$

$$R_f \text{ of } C = \frac{8}{40} = 0.20$$

Figure 7—Chromatogram

Conclusions

1. When you compared the chromatograms of the different samples, what did you observe? What conclusions can be drawn from your results?

2. If possible, calculate the RF values for your chromatograms.

52

 **SOLVE**

Forensic Activity: Attempted Abduction

The victim, Angora Barathea, was walking to work when a black van pulled up beside her. A man jumped out and lifted her quickly into the van, which sped off. Ms. Barathea was pushed face first into the carpeting and blindfolded, and her hands were tied behind her back. The assailants soon stopped for beer at a party store. Angora managed to kick her way out of the van and ran screaming for help. The van drove off.

Within the hour, a black van with three men inside was stopped. They were identified as Dimity Crimp, Chino Stitch, and Buckram Blotch. Police impounded the vehicle and arrested the three on suspicion of assault and kidnapping. Stuffed beneath a seat was a rag of the same color as the blindfold and strip used to tie Angora's hands.

1. Each investigative group will receive a package of evidence with three envelopes containing fabric. Your job is to ascertain if the cloth from the van is the same as that used to blindfold and tie Angora Barathea. A Crime Report form must be independently completed by each investigator in each group, with the realization that any one member of the group may be called as an expert witness at trial. Therefore, any conclusions must be justified and able to withstand cross-examination.

2. What other forensic evidence might be found to link the suspects to the abduction?

3. How would you determine the probability of a random match of cloth of the same color and composition as found in the van (i.e., what are the odds that another black van in the area had a similar rag)?

CRIME REPORT

CASE NO. _____ DATE _____

NATURE OF CRIME _____

DATE OF OCCURENCE _____

TIME OF OCCURENCE _____

LOCATION _____

VICTIM _____

BRIEF HISTORY OF CASE:

TYPE OF EVIDENCE SUBMITTED FOR EXAMINATION _____
List each individual item: use Q for questioned (source unknown);
K for known (source established).

BRIEF DESCRIPTION OF METHODS USED:

CASE NO. _____

RESULTS:

CONCLUSIONS:

SIGNATURE _____ DATE _____

NAME OF INVESTIGATIVE GROUP _____

BACKGROUND

Blood as Forensic Evidence

What Is Blood?

Approximately one-twelfth of the human body is blood, which is basically cells suspended in a liquid. The fluid portion is called **plasma** (55% of the blood). It is composed of 90% water and 10% **metabolites**—waste, salts, ions (mostly Na^+, Cl^- HCO_3^-), and proteins. The solid portion of blood is composed of three principal types of cells: (1) Red (**erythrocytes**), which contain hemoglobin, transport oxygen from the lungs to the cells and in return carry carbon dioxide back to the lungs, where it is exhaled. (2) White cells (**leukocytes**) are the primary cells of the immune system. They produce antibodies. (3) **Platelets** start the clotting process by initiating the formation of fibrin to form a clot. Removing the solid clotting material leaves a pale yellow, watery fluid called **serum**.

In 1901, Austrian biologist Karl Landsteiner recognized that all human blood was not the same and worked out the **ABO classification system** to describe the differences. This was important because so many blood transfusions had resulted in immediate death of the patient for no apparent reason. In 1940, Landsteiner discovered the **rhesus factor (Rh)** in blood. Now over 100 different factors are known to exist. Theoretically, no one, except identical twins, has the same combination of **blood factors**; practically, however, the complete identification is difficult, time-consuming, and expensive. Also, many factors break down as blood dries and ages. In the forensic-science world, blood-factor identification is not yet practical as a means of individualization. DNA analysis, on the other hand, offers individualization, but also is time-consuming and expensive. Nevertheless, ABO and Rh blood characterization is an important component of forensic serology because it can be done on whole blood as well as dried blood stains, quickly and without expensive apparatus. Additionally, about 80% of the population are **secretors**, meaning their blood-type antigens are found in body fluids other than just blood.

Present on the surface of each red blood cell (RBC) are millions of characteristic chemical structures called **antigens**. These proteins are responsible for the different blood types. For the ABO system, there are two types of antigens, A and B. Type A blood cells have

> **Approximately one-twelfth of the human body is blood.**

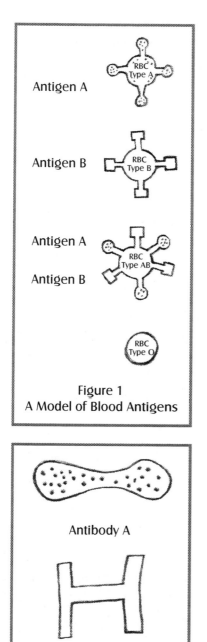

Figure 1
A Model of Blood Antigens

Antibody A

Antibody B

Figure 2
A Model of Blood Antibodies

A antigens, type B blood cells have B antigens, type AB blood cells have both A and B antigens, and type O blood cells have neither antigen.

Some white blood cells manufacture proteins called **antibodies** that are found in the **serum**, the yellowish liquid that separates from blood when a clot is formed. These antibodies, known as **antiserum**, are produced to attack invaders that enter the blood stream (antigens that do not belong in your system, such as snake venom, bacteria, or someone else's blood). For example, when viruses responsible for the mumps enter the blood, the body recognizes them as foreign and begins synthesizing antibodies that combine only with the specific antigens of the virus. Antibody-coated viruses are destroyed by white blood cells. If the person is again exposed to mumps, the existing antibodies are able to prevent a repetition of the illness. This is the basis of vaccines.

A person with type A blood (A antigens on their red blood cells) will produce specific antibodies in their serum to attack and destroy type B blood cells as they are introduced into the body. Type A's serum containing the B antibodies is called anti-B antibodies or anti-B serum, because it destroys type B blood cells. Likewise, a person with type B blood will have A antibodies in their serum. Type AB blood has both A and B antigens on the red blood cells and no antibodies in the serum. Type O blood, which has neither A nor B antigens, has anti-A and anti-B antibodies in its serum. This is confusing—you may have to think about it for a while to fully understand. Table 1 provides a summary of blood types.

TABLE 1 Blood Types		
Blood Type	**Antigens on RBC**	**Antibodies in Serum**
A	A	anti-B
B	B	anti-A
AB	A and B	none
O	none	anti-A and anti-B

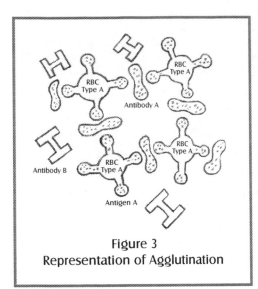

Figure 3
Representation of Agglutination

Antibodies are **bivalent,** which means that they can attach to two antigen sites, thus causing **agglutination,** or clumping, similar to cross-linking in polymers. If a person with type B blood receives a transfusion of type A blood, the anti-A antibodies in the recipient's B blood will attach to the donor's A red blood cells and cause agglutination, as depicted in Figure 3.

The result can be fatal. This is why ABO typing is necessary before undergoing blood transfusions. The anti-B antibodies received from the donor are diluted by the larger volume of the recipient's blood, so the transfused antibodies do not cause a problem. Table 2 shows safe blood-donor and recipient combinations.

TABLE 2 Safe ABO Combinations				
Blood Type	**Antigen**	**Antibody**	**Donor For**	**Recipient For**
A	A	anti-B	A, AB	A, O
B	B	anti-A	B, AB	B, O
AB	A & B	none	AB	all
O	none	anti-A & anti-B	all	O

The Rh factor is another important means of classifying blood type for forensic **serology.** It is sometimes referred to as the D antigen. Those who have it are called Rh positive (Rh+); those without it, Rh negative (Rh−). Approximately 85% of the population is Rh+.

The distribution of blood type varies both with location and race throughout the world. In the United States, a typical ABO distribution is illustrated in Table 3.

TABLE 3	
Blood Type	**Percentage**
Type A	41
Type B	10
Type AB	4
Type O	45

Thus, blood typing can be important in forensic science because it can show that two samples did not have the same origin; that is, typing evidence can exclude suspects. Also, the distribution of blood types within a specific population can be used to statistically determine the probability of someone having a particular combination of blood types. For example, what is the probability of a person having type B+ blood?

$$\frac{10}{100} \times \frac{85}{100} = \frac{850}{10,000} \text{ or about 1 out of 12 people.}$$

Exploration Activities

1. What is the probability of a person having type AB– blood? Show your calculations.

2. Blood typing can be applied to a host of enzymes and proteins that perform specific functions in the body. Their presence or absence varies within the population. More than 150 serum proteins and 250 cellular enzymes have been isolated. Therefore, it is possible to use blood typing as individual evidence; however, it is not practical to achieve the statistics required because of the time and techniques involved. Also, most factors degrade with time. Rather, ABO/Rh typing, and often another kind of typing called MNS, are used as exclusionary tests in forensic science and paternity testing. The typical population in the United States shows an MNS distribution of M = 30%, N = 27%, S = 48%. If a blood stain found at the scene of a crime is found to be B, N, Rh–, what are the chances that a suspect would have this combination of antigens? Is this good enough to convince a jury?

3. How much blood is there in the average adult human?

LAB

Student Lab: Detection of Blood

Is It Blood?

A red-brown stain is found on a piece of fabric. Maybe it is blood, maybe paint, or ketchup, or food coloring, or rust, or . . . .

Materials

- Stained fabric samples
- Hand lens or stereomicroscope
- Filter paper

- **Hematest**® tablets or **Hemastix**® strips
- Kastle-Meyer reagent
- Hydrogen peroxide

Procedure

1. Observe the different samples of what may be blood stains on a piece of fabric. Use a hand lens or stereomicroscope if necessary. Record appearance and what you think each stain is and why (color, shape, smell, texture, etc.).

There are several **presumptive tests** of chemical color that can be used to detect the presence of blood.

- Commercial blood testing reagent—The hem in **hemoglobin** catalytically decomposes **peroxides** with the evolution of oxygen. Oxygen reacts with a chemical in the **Hematest**™ tablet or **Hemastix**™ test strip to turn it blue.

2. Press a piece of wet filter paper on an area of the stained cloth that you think is most likely to be blood. Break a Hematest™ tablet into quarters. Place one portion of the tablet in the center of the transferred stain on the filter paper and add a drop of water *onto the tablet*. Make sure the water flows down the side of the tablet onto the stain. A blue-green ring spreading out on the filter paper from the tablet indicates the spot is blood. A Hemastix™ strip can be rubbed on the wet stain with a green to blue color denoting the presence of blood. Substances other than blood, such as dry bleach residues and some plastics, can cause similar results. Run a blank test on an unstained area of the filter paper. Record your results. If the stain did not react as positive to what you thought was blood, repeat until you get the desired result. Attach your filter paper(s) to a separate sheet of paper.

- The **Kastle-Meyer** color test, like the Hematest™ just completed, is based on the catalytic decomposition of peroxides by hemoglobin. When reduced phenolphthalein reagent and hydrogen peroxide contact a blood stain, a deep pink color is formed. Unfortunately, there are several substances that give a **false-positive**, such as potatoes and horse radish. A false positive is a test result that comes out positive when it is not.

3. Press a piece of wet filter paper on the blood stain on the cloth. Add a drop of K-M reagent to the paper where it contacted the stain, and then add a drop of 3% hydrogen peroxide. Repeat on an unstained area as a control. Record your results.

- The **luminol test** is a very sensitive indicator for dried and even washed blood. Spraying a suspected area with luminol reagent can be achieved quickly and cause even old blood stains to glow (**chemiluminesce**). The area must be very dark and your eyes conditioned to the darkness in order to see the luminescence. False positives can be caused by certain metals (Cu, Fe, Co), bleach, and sometimes even plaster walls. If your teacher demonstrates the use of luminol, record your observations.

Conclusion

1. Define a presumptive test.

 **LAB**

Student Lab: Testing Human or Animal Blood

So if It Is Blood, Is It Human or Animal Blood?

After a stain has been determined to be blood, the next step is to determine if it is human or animal blood. The **precipitin test** is the standard method. It uses an animal serum that contains antibodies specific to human antigens; therefore, it reacts to agglutinate human blood. The test is so sensitive that the blood can be diluted a great deal. Also, bloodstains many years old can be tested.

Materials

- Human anti-serum
- Simulated blood sample
- Test tube
- Pipets

Blood is typed by mixing it with serum containing known antibodies and looking for agglutination.

Procedure

1. Add to a small test tube about 1 cm of simulated human anti-serum. Carefully pour the same amount of a diluted simulated blood sample down the sides of the test tube so as not to disturb the bottom layer. Agglutination will occur at the interface of the two liquids if the blood is human. Be patient—sometimes it takes a while. Record your observations. The contents of the test tube can be discarded down the drain.

Blood is tested for type by mixing a drop of blood with a drop of serum containing known antibodies. The presence or absence of agglutination allows selection of blood type in the ABO system.

Conclusion

1. What three questions should an investigator answer when examining an apparent dried blood stain?

 **SOLVE**

Forensic Activity: Assault

Johnny Appleseed has been mugged on his way back from the orchard. He managed to slash his attacker with his paring knife. Fresh blood is collected from leaves at the scene. Eight suspects, each with a bandaged arm, are rounded up by the police, but none can be positively identified by Mr. Appleseed because it was getting dark at the time of the attack. Blood samples from the crime scene and the suspects are delivered with the request for immediate typing because the police can't hold the suspects for very long. The blood type for Mr. Appleseed has been taken from his blood donor card and is type A−.

Note: No blood or blood products will be used in this lab. This is merely a simulation of the reactions that take place in the typing of blood, where actual human blood and human antisera are used.

Procedure

1. Place a slide under the stereomicroscope and focus, or use a hand lens.

2. Add three drops of Suspect 1 blood to the slide, side by side, making sure that they do not touch each other.

3. Add one drop of anti-A to the first drop of blood.

4. Add one drop of anti-B to the second drop of blood.

5. Add one drop of anti-Rh to the third drop of blood.

6. Mix the cells and the antisera with a toothpick, watching to see if agglutination takes place. Be sure to clean the toothpick between drops to avoid contamination.

7. Use Table 4 to determine the blood type and Rh factor of Suspect 1.

8. Repeat the procedure for all the suspects and the sample from the crime scene.

TABLE 4 Agglutination Reactions		
If Anti-A	**and Anti-B**	**then blood type is**
+	−	A
−	+	B
+	+	AB
−	−	O

+ means agglutination occurs; − no agglutination

The Rh factor is either present or not present; agglutination indicates its presence; no reaction indicates its absence.

Conclusions

1. Record your results in the crime report and complete it accordingly. Remember, you may be called as an expert witness at trial. Therefore, any conclusions must be justified and able to withstand cross-examination.

2. On the way to the police department for questioning, suspect Jonathan Gold was in a severe car accident and needed a blood transfusion. Which of the other suspects could be donors for him?

3. How many people in the general population would have the same blood type as suspect 4?

4. Which suspects could receive a transfusion of type AB blood?

5. Which blood type is known as the universal donor? Why can this blood type donate to all others?

6. Which blood type is known as the universal receiver? Why can this blood type receive all others safely?

7. If you have type B+ blood, what type(s) can you receive?

Real blood that has been dried can still be typed. The red blood cells have been ruptured, but the antigens and antibodies are still present. In subsequent crime scenes that you may encounter, the standard typing procedure can be used for the simulated blood.

Packaging and storage of blood evidence should not exclude air; a sealed container may trap any moisture present and cause the formation of mold and mildew.

8. Can a bloodstain be used for individualization? Explain.

FORENSIC SCIENCE UNIT

CRIME REPORT

CASE NO. ________________ DATE ______

NATURE OF CRIME ____________________

DATE OF OCCURENCE ____________________

TIME OF OCCURENCE ____________________

LOCATION ____

VICTIM ____

BRIEF HISTORY OF CASE:

TYPE OF EVIDENCE SUBMITTED FOR EXAMINATION ____________________
List each individual item: use Q for questioned (source unknown);
K for known (source established).

BRIEF DESCRIPTION OF METHODS USED:

CASE NO. _____

RESULTS:

Suspect #	Name	Anti-A	Anti-B	Anti-Rh	Bloodtype
1	Angus McIntosh				
2	Arthur Redwell				
3	Robert Braeburn				
4	Jonathan Gold				
5	Phillip Macoun				
6	Baldwin Sapp				
7	Mortimer Gravenstein				
8	Jimmy Jon Gala				
9	Crime Scene				

CONCLUSIONS:

SIGNATURE _____ DATE _____

NAME OF INVESTIGATIVE GROUP _____

66

BACKGROUND

Blood Spatter Analysis

What Does Blood Spatter Analysis Mean?

Blood Spatter Analysis is a field of forensic science that deals with the physical properties of blood and the patterns produced under different conditions as a result of various forces applied to the source of blood. The patterns left by falling, projected, or smeared blood can help the forensic investigator interpret and reconstruct what has happened at a crime scene. Blood spatter patterns are often used to corroborate or refute the suspect's account of what happened. Careful observation of the position and shape of stain patterns can give information such as the direction of travel, the angle of impact, the position of origin, and the blood droplet's speed at the time of impact.

Note that it is "spatter," not "splatter." And not all blood spatter is flung blood.

Early on the morning of July 4, 1954, police received a call from Dr. Sam Sheppard. He reported that his wife, Marilyn, was dead in their bedroom in their two-story lakefront home. He explained to police that the night before, Marilyn had left him on the couch and went to sleep in the twin bed next to Sam's. He fell asleep and awoke some time later, believing he heard his wife calling his name. He went upstairs and saw Marilyn covered with blood. He checked for her pulse and found none. Sheppard heard a noise below, ran downstairs and saw a form moving toward the lake. He chased the person across the lawn and down the steps leading to the beach. He struggled with a man, 6'3", middle aged, with dark bushy hair and a white shirt. Sheppard was choked to unconsciousness. Marilyn had 35 wounds to the head; blood drenched the walls, door, and bed where she lay. Her face was almost unrecognizable.

Sheppard served 10 years in prison before the U.S. Supreme Court ruled that his trial was tainted. The evidence was re-examined; blood spatters in the bedroom and blood drops throughout the house gave some of the most telling evidence. The expert, Dr. Paul Kirks, concluded that the killer could not have been Sheppard based on the fact that the killer was left handed. Dr. Sheppard was right handed.

> ## The patterns left by blood can help in crime scene reconstruction.

Student Lab: Blood Pattern Analysis

Develop a procedure for the analysis and interpretation of bloodstains. Be sure to make accurate observations, measurements and sketches, and to record all data.

Materials

- Wide roll of paper
- Simulated blood
- Pipettes
- Writing paper

- Plastic knife or tongue depressor
- Protractor, ruler, meter stick
- String
- Masking tape

Answer the following questions:

- •What is the effect of release height on the pattern left by drops of blood?

- •What is the effect of velocity on impact patterns?

- •How does the angle of impact affect the appearance of drops of blood?

- •How is the direction of travel determined from a blood pattern?

- •How can it be determined that an assailant is right or left handed?

- •How can the origin of blood spatter be determined?

Remember, you may be called upon to evaluate a crime scene that will require your expertise, and your notes will be your only reference.

BACKGROUND

Glass as Forensic Evidence

How Can Glass Be Used as Evidence?

Glass fragments found at a crime scene can be used to place a suspect at the scene. The fragments may be found in a suspect's clothing or embedded in shoes as a result of breaking a window to gain entry to a house, or they may be found on a victim of a hit-and-run. If the fragments can be pieced together, like the pieces of a jigsaw puzzle, the evidence can be individualized (see Figure 1). Most often, however, glass shatters into so many fragments that piecing them together is impossible; thus it must be considered as class evidence.

It is the task of the forensic scientist to use as many physical properties of glass as possible to characterize the fragments and associate the fragments from the crime scene to a suspect. Also, by studying the fracture patterns of glass, a sequence of events can be deduced to aid in the reconstruction of a crime.

What Is Glass?

Glass is a very common material found in our environment. It is a hard, **amorphous** material, usually transparent, composed primarily of silica (SiO_2) and various amounts of element oxides. It is brittle and exhibits **conchoidal** fracture. Glass can be classified into families (**taxonomy**) like many other materials you have studied. The families differ widely in chemical composition and physical properties (See Table 1). There is far less variation of properties within families.

Many of the properties of glass cannot be measured from small fragments and are of little concern to the forensic scientist. Most important are **density** and **refractive index**. Color, thickness, fluorescence, and of course, any extraordinary markings, such as striations, dimples, and so on, may be helpful. Modern instrumentation, such as **neutron activation analysis** and **ICP (inductively coupled plasma) spectrometry**, allow routine determination of trace elements in glass. This may eventually lead to a unique "fingerprint" for each batch manufactured.

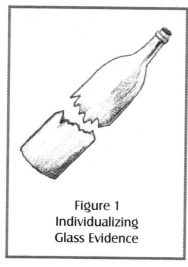
Figure 1
Individualizing
Glass Evidence

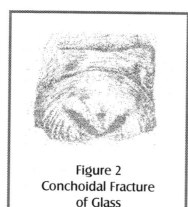
Figure 2
Conchoidal Fracture
of Glass

TABLE 1 Composition of Glasses

Composition of Representative Oxide Glasses

Glass Family	Glass Application	Oxide Ingredient (Percent by Weight)									
		silica (SiO$_2$)	soda (Na$_2$O)	lime (CaO)	alumina (Al$_2$O$_2$)	magnesia (MgO)	boron oxide (B$_2$O$_3$)	barium oxide (BaO)	lead oxid (PbO)	potassium oxide (K$_2$O)	zinc oxide (ZnO)
Vitreus Silica	furnace tubes, silicon melting crucibles	100.0									
Soda-lime silicate	window	72.0	14.2	10.0	0.5	2.5					
	container	74.0	15.3	5.4	1.0	3.7				0.6	
	bulb and tube	73.3	16.0	5.2	1.3	3.5				0.6	
	tableware	74.0	18.0	7.5	0.5			trace			
Sodium borosilicate	chemical glassware	81.0	4.5		2.0		12.0				
Lead-alkali silicate	lead "crystal"	59.0	2.0		0.4				25.0	12.0	1.5
	television funnel	54.0	6.0	3.0	2.0	2.0			23.0	8.0	
Aluminosilicate	glass halogen lamp	57.0	0.01	10.0	16.0	7.0	4.0	6.0		trace	
	fiberglass "E"	52.9		17.4	14.5	4.4	9.2			1.0	
Optical	"crown"	68.9	8.8				10.1	2.8		8.4	1.0

 **LAB**

Student Lab: Examination of Glass Pieces

Materials

- Glass samples of different sizes
- UV light
- Stereomicroscope
- Ruler

Special Safety Considerations

Handle glass pieces with care, as they may be sharp. Long-wave UV light sources emit at 366 nm (UVA band). While they may cause eye damage over long exposures, it is still not a good idea to look directly into the light even for short periods. Short-wavelength UV light sources, those used for mineral fluorescence, emit at 254 nm (UVC) and are extremely hazardous, causing loss of vision and cataracts.

Procedure

1. Make a list of where glass materials are used or found. Brainstorm with your Investigative Group and think of as many different uses for glass as you can.

2. Examine samples of known glass pieces that your teacher has provided. Use both long- and short-wave UV light to determine which ones fluoresce. Be sure to note subtle differences. Note any glasses that fluoresce, observing the color and intensity.

3. Color is difficult to identify in small, thin fragments of glass. Use reflected light with a stereomicroscope or a good magnifying lens to examine samples of small fragments.

Conclusions

1. What are some ways that glass materials are used?

2. Which glasses fluoresce? What color and intensity does each fluoresce?

3. Based on your observations, consider the physical properties that can be used to compare glass samples. List them.

4. Describe the color of each sample you observed in step 3 of the Procedure section.

5. Thickness may vary greatly in a bottle, yet be quite uniform in plate glass. Estimate the thickness of the original glass from fragments large enough to show smooth, parallel sides.

6. Perhaps you noted fluorescence in some of your macroscopic samples. This is seldom a useful indicator in fragments. Exceptions may be uranium glass, lead glass ("crystal"), and some quartz glasses. Do any fragment samples fluoresce? What are they?

Student Lab: Measuring the Density of a Glass Fragment

> **Density is defined as mass per unit volume. The ratio of the density of a substance to that of water is called specific gravity.**

The simplest way of measuring density of glass is called the **flotation method**. It is based on the observation that a solid particle will float in a liquid medium of greater density, sink in a liquid of lower density, or remain suspended in a liquid of equal density. We will use a mixture of bromoform (d = 2.89 g/cm^3) and bromobenzene (d = 1.52 g/cm^3).

TABLE 2 Density of Various Materials, in g/cm^3			
Window glass	2.46–2.49	Diamond	3.52
Headlight glass	2.47–2.63	Sugar	1.59
Optical glass	2.64–2.81	Salt	2.17
Vitreous silica glass	2.2	KClO$_4$	2.52
Quartz	2.65	MgSO$_4$	2.66
Pyrex glass	2.23–2.36	Aluminum	2.7
Lead glass	2.9–5.9	Iron	7.9
Porcelain	2.3–2.5	Lead	11.3
Water	1.0	Plastics	0.9–2.2

Materials

- Glass fragments
- Bromoform
- Bromobenzene
- Beral or Pasteur pipets

- Tweezers
- Test tubes with rack or holder
- Stirring rods

Special Safety Considerations

Handle glass pieces with care, as they may be sharp. Both bromoform and bromobenzene are slightly toxic. Work in a well-ventilated area and wash your hands after using them.

73

Procedure

1. Working in the hood or by the window, use your tweezers to place a small (~1–2-mm) fragment of glass in a 10-cm or smaller test tube.

2. Using a beral or Pasteur pipet, add enough drops of bromoform to fill the test tube about a quarter full. Count the drops and record the number. The glass should float on the surface of the liquid.

3. Now add bromobenzene, drop by drop. You want to adjust the density of the liquid in the test tube so that the fragment is suspended. Use a stirring rod to mix the two liquids before observing the location of the glass each time. Record the number of drops of bromobenzene needed.

4. The density of the mixture of bromoform and bromobenzene can be calculated according to the following equation:

$$D = \frac{X(2.89) + Y(1.52)}{X + Y}$$

Where D = density
X = drops of bromoform
Y = drops of bromobenzene

5. Without disturbing your density tube, add a different sample. You need not stir this time. Note where the sample comes to equilibrium.

Conclusions

1. Why does the glass fragment float on the surface of the liquid in step 1 of the Procedure section?

2. Calculate the density of your glass fragment. Compare with other results.

3. Is the sample you added in step 5 heavier or lighter than the original sample? What kind of glass could it be? How could you easily determine its density?

 **BACKGROUND**

Refractive Index

> **Refractive index is a physical property of any material that will transmit light.**

Light travels in straight lines at approximately 300,000,000 meters per second in air. When it strikes the surface of a transparent material, such as glass, it can be reflected, absorbed, and transmitted. When light passes from one medium into another, there is a change in its direction and velocity. This phenomenon is called **refraction**. Light traveling from a less dense substance to a more dense substance (as from air to glass) will slow down. The refractive index (n) is a comparison of the speed of light in a vacuum to the speed of light in another substance.

$$n(\text{air}) = 1.0003$$

For example, the speed of light in water is 225,000,000 meters per second; its refractive index can be calculated as:

$$\frac{3.00 \times 10^8}{2.25 \times 10^8} = 1.33$$

Refractive index is a physical property of any substance that will transmit light. If a clear material, such as glass, is immersed in a liquid that has the same refractive index, both the glass and the liquid will bend light at the same angle, and the glass will appear to disappear!

75

 **LAB**

Student Lab: Determining Refractive Index

Materials

- Optics kit
- Protractor
- Sine table
- Test substances provided by teacher
- CRC *Handbook of Chemistry and Physics*

Procedure

1. Set up a light box so that a single, thin beam of light passes over a piece of scrap paper. Place a rectangular piece of glass on the grid below with one edge along the horizontal line. Shine the beam of light at an angle so that it hits the rectangular piece of glass at the center cross. Trace the outside of the glass and the path of light as it travels toward the glass and through the glass (but not on the other side of the glass), Figure 1.

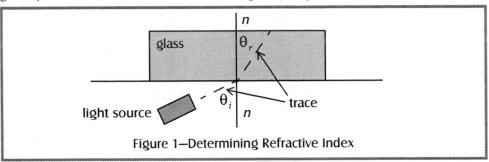

Figure 1—Determining Refractive Index

2. Measure and record the two angles: **angle of incidence**, θ_i, and **angle of refraction**, θ_r. Both angles must be measured from the normal (n), a line that is perpendicular to the surface of the glass.

3. Measure the refractive index using **Snell's law**:

$$\frac{\sin\theta_I}{\sin\theta_r} = n \text{ (refractive index)}$$

4. Repeat #3 for several *different* angles and record your data. Investigate what happens with very small incident angles and very large incident angles. Make drawings similar to Figure 1.

5. Investigate how different materials affect how light is refracted. Try passing a light beam through water, different types of glass and plastic, vegetable oil, corn syrup, or whatever substances are available. Make a table for the data.

Conclusions

1. Look at your data for step 4 in the Procedure section. What conclusions can you make?

2. Why do you think light bends when it travels from air to glass?

3. Do you think water would cause the light to bend more or less than glass? Why?

4. How could you test this? In what other type of substances would light behave like this?

5. Calculate refractive indices for all the materials you tested. Make a table and include values from your classmates.

6. Compare these values to the published values in the CRC *Handbook of Chemistry and Physics*. Explain any differences.

 **LAB**

Student Lab: Refractive Index of Glass Fragments

Why is the refractive index of glass important in forensic science?

Refractive index (RI, also designated as n_D, where the subscript D refers to a particular wavelength of light used in the measurement), like density, is a property of glass that, coupled with other properties, may increase the probability of finding a common origin between a known and unknown sample—provided, of course, that different types of glass have different indices. The **histogram** shown in Figure 2 depicts the variation, and possible confusion, in this property of glass. Rather sophisticated apparatus is needed to find the refractive index of materials to five significant figures.

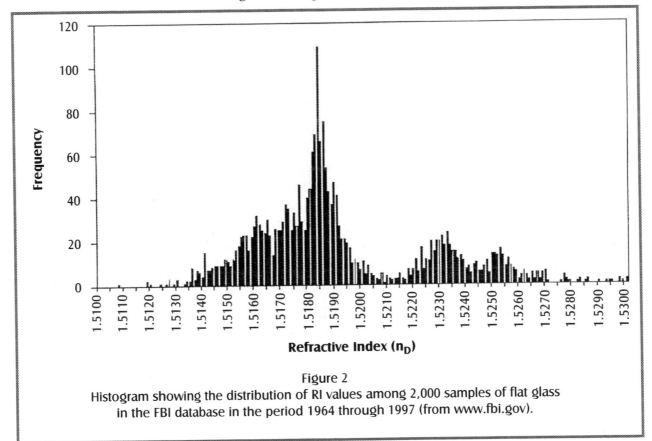

Figure 2
Histogram showing the distribution of RI values among 2,000 samples of flat glass in the FBI database in the period 1964 through 1997 (from www.fbi.gov).

To compare fragments of glass, we can use the fact that glass will seem to disappear when immersed in a liquid of the same refractive index.

Materials

- Glass fragments
- Hand lens
- Alcohol
- Beakers
- Watch glasses
- Forceps or tweezers
- Refractive index liquids

Procedure

1. Select a glass fragment about 1–2 mm, as thin or flat as possible. Immerse it entirely in each of the selected refractive index oils, observing it with a good hand lens.

2. Remove it from the liquid with forceps, rinse it in alcohol, and blot it dry between each immersion. Record the refractive index that most closely approximates each sample that the teacher has given you.

3. Table 3 lists refractive indices for a number of materials. Compare your RI values with the values listed in the table.

TABLE 3 Refractive Indices			
Methanol	1.329	Vitreous silica	1.458
Water	1.333	Pyrex®	1.47
Isopropanol	1.377	Headlight glass	1.47–1.49
Olive oil	1.467	Television glass	1.49–1.51
Glycerin	1.473	Window glass	1.51–1.52
Castor oil	1.482	Bottle glass	1.51–1.52
Canadian balsam	1.54	Acrylic polymer	1.52
Clove oil	1.543	Optical glass	1.52–1.53
Bromobenzene	1.560	Aluminosilicate	1.547
Bromoform	1.597	Quartz	1.544–1.553
Cinnamon oil	1.619	Lead glass	1.56–1.61
		Diamond	2.419

Conclusions

1. Analyze the histogram. Which has more probative value, a glass fragment with a RI of 1.5145, or one with RI of 1.5193? Why? What are the odds of finding one over the other?

2. Is there a significant difference between the RI values that you recorded for each sample and the refractive indices listed in Table 3? Why?

Forensic Activity: Burglary

A burglary is committed by breaking the window in the back door of a house to allow the thief to reach in and unlock the door. The back hallway has no carpet. A suspect is apprehended and his living quarters searched. A few small glass fragments are found embedded in the soles of his sneakers. The suspect works in a body shop and explains that there is always broken headlight glass on the shop floor. The small fragments of glass recovered from the suspect's shoes may be associated to the crime scene or the body shop by means of comparing certain physical properties of glass.

1. Each Investigative Group will receive a package of evidence containing three containers of glass fragments. Your job is to ascertain if the evidence submitted can associate the suspect to the burglary. A Crime Report form must be independently completed by each investigator in each group, with the realization that any one member of the group may be called as an expert witness at trial. Therefore, any conclusions must be justified and able to withstand cross-examination.

2. Does the evidence show that the suspect committed the burglary?

3. What other forensic evidence might be found to link the suspect to the theft?

4. You are on the stand as an expert witness in the comparative analysis of glass fragments. You must define and explain to the jury (generally consider a jury equivalent to a seventh-grade level) the following terms:

   a. fluorescence

   b. density and specific gravity

   c. reflection and refraction

   d. refractive index

   e. class evidence

   f. under what circumstances glass evidence could be individualized

CRIME REPORT

CASE NO. _____ DATE _____

NATURE OF CRIME _____

DATE OF OCCURENCE _____

TIME OF OCCURENCE _____

LOCATION _____

VICTIM _____

BRIEF HISTORY OF CASE:

TYPE OF EVIDENCE SUBMITTED FOR EXAMINATION _____
List each individual item: use Q for questioned (source unknown);
K for known (source established).

BRIEF DESCRIPTION OF METHODS USED:

CASE NO. _____

RESULTS:

CONCLUSIONS:

SIGNATURE _____ DATE _____

NAME OF INVESTIGATIVE GROUP _____

 **BACKGROUND**

Fracture Patterns

What Happens to a Pane of Glass When a Projectile Strikes It?

> **Fracture patterns in glass can be used as forensic evidence.**

Information about the events of a crime scene can sometimes be constructed by fracture patterns of glass. How the cracks are formed, what shape they have, whether or not the breakage was caused on the inside or outside, are clues as to what happened.

> In a California case, a wounded suspect claimed he was fired upon by an officer and only returned fire in self-defense. The shots had penetrated the windshield of the suspect's car. By studying the cracks and the inside-outside size of the holes, it was established that the suspect fired at the officer first.
> —from David Fisher, *Hard Evidence*

Glass is slightly flexible, but when forced to its elastic limit, it will break or fracture. Studying the break or fracture pattern will provide information on the force and direction. Glass's elasticity also causes some glass fragments to recoil backward (**blowback**) toward the direction of force, thus possibly providing clues in the perpetrator's clothing, hair, and other features.

When glass is broken with a projectile, such as a bullet or rock, it will form two distinct types of fractures, **radial** and **concentric**. Figure 3, on the next page, shows how the radial and concentric fractures occur. When a projectile first hits the glass, the glass will be stretched, causing tension on the back side directly behind the projectile. This causes compression around the point of tension. The radial cracks begin on the opposite side of the force at the point where the projectile hits the glass (A) and radiate out from the origin of the impact. The concentric cracks begin on the same side as the force, where the tension occurs (B).

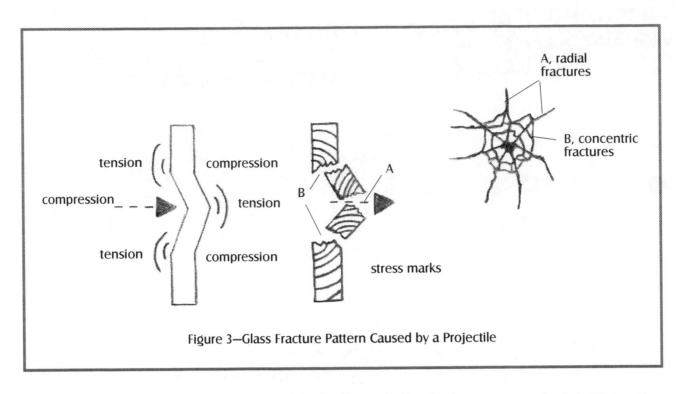

Figure 3—Glass Fracture Pattern Caused by a Projectile

Visible at the edge of broken glass are stress marks (see Figure 3). They are shaped like arches with the perpendicular at the surface where the crack originated. Thus, examination of the edges of a glass fragment that can be fitted into the mosaic of a broken window allows determination of the direction of impact. Also, a high-velocity projectile always leaves a hole wider at the exit side of the glass. The size of the hole itself is not necessarily indicative of the size of the projectile.

Exploration Activities

1. Figure 4 shows two bullet holes in a window glass. A second fracture will always terminate when it meets an existing line of fracture. Which hole was made first?

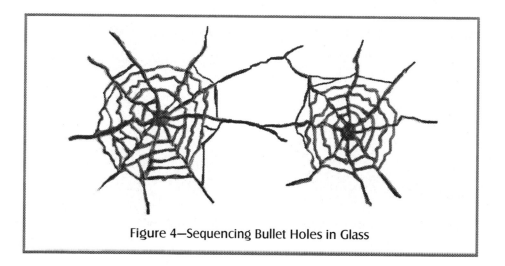

Figure 4—Sequencing Bullet Holes in Glass

2. Label the radial and concentric fractures in Figure 4.

Student Lab: Analysis of Glass Fracture Patterns

Holes in a window, or any enclosure for that matter, can sometimes be used to pinpoint the location of the shooter if a projectile leaves a second mark at some length behind the first one. For example, fixing a laser pointer at the second mark so that the beam shines through the initial hole illuminates a probable point of origin. Factors affecting trajectory, such as wind, distance, and types of projectile, must be taken into account.

Materials

- Panes of glass with holes

Procedure

Study the panes of glass provided and determine where the projectile hit the glass (front or back), and which hole was made first. Draw a picture on a separate sheet of paper, recording all observations.

Conclusion

1. Where did the projectile hit the glass? Were you able to determine which hole was made first? How?

 **BACKGROUND**

Soil as Forensic Evidence

Is Soil the Same as Dirt, Earth, or Ground?

Like so many words, the definition of *soil* depends on where you are coming from. As with dirt, earth, and ground, soil is defined in many ways:

- By the generalist—Soil is the surface of the earth that is not water, air, or rock.

- In a dictionary—Soil is material in the top layer of the surface of the earth in which plants can grow.

- By a farmer—Soil is the upper layer of earth that may be dug or plowed and in which plants grow.

- By an engineer—Soil is all the fragmented mineral material at or near the surface of the earth, the moon, or other planetary bodies, plus the air, water, organic matter, and other substances that may be included therein.

- By a planetary scientist—Soil is material at the surface of planets and similar bodies altered by biologic, chemical, and/ or physical agents.

- By a soil scientist—Soil is a natural body composed of solids (minerals and organic matter), liquid, and gases that occurs on the land surface, occupies space, and is characterized by one or both of the following: horizons, or layers, that are distinguishable from the initial material as a result of additions, losses, transfers, and transformations of energy and matter or the ability to support rooted plants in a natural environment.

- By the FBI—Soil is the natural accumulation of weathering rocks, minerals, and decomposing plants. Soil may contain synthetic materials such as brick, roof shingle stones, concrete, glass, and paint.

Soil Evidence

A seamstress named Eva Disch was found in a bean field strangled with her own scarf. Nasal mucus on a dirty handkerchief left at the scene of the crime contained bits of coal, particles of snuff, and

> **To the FBI soil is the natural accumulation of weathering rocks, minerals, and decomposing plants, and it may contain synthetic materials.**

small mineral grains, particularly horneblende. A suspect, Karl Laubach, was known to work in a coal-burning gasworks and part-time in a local gravel pit. The investigator, a man named Georg Popp, found coal and mineral grains under Mr. Laubach's finger-nails. The suspect was also known to use snuff.

Examination of Laubach's pants revealed a layer of soil, in direct contact with the fabric of the pants leg, containing the very same minerals as found in the soil where the body of Ms. Disch was recovered. A different type of soil coated the first layer of mud on Laubach's pants. The mineralogy, in particular the presence of mica, was comparable to the suspect's house. From these data, Popp concluded that Mr. Laubach had picked up the first layer of soil at the crime scene and the outer layer on his return home.

When Mr. Laubach was confronted with the soil evidence, he confessed to the murder. This crime was committed in Germany in October 1904 and is the first recorded use of forensic geology!

[Abstracted from *Forensic Geology,* by Raymond C. Murray and John C. F. Tedrow.]

Student Lab: Examination of Soil

How Can Soil Be Useful as Forensic Evidence?

If all soil were the same, it would be like matching white cotton fibers to a common source. In this lab, we will see if all soil is the same.

Materials

- Wet soil sample
- Dry soil sample (dried overnight by your teacher)
- Notebook paper
- Stereomicroscope
- Petri dishes

Procedure

1. Dump the sample of wet soil on a clean sheet of white notebook paper. Note its features.

2. Rub a little of the soil into the paper with a wet finger. Note the color before and after it has dried. Place the sample back in the container.

3. Place a portion of your dried soil sample in a clear plastic or glass petri dish. Examine it under a stereomicroscope with transmitted as well as reflected light. Pay special attention to any synthetic artifacts as described in the FBI definition of soil. Observe any once-living organisms.

4. Compare the description of your soil sample, wet and dry, to the descriptions made by classmates.

Conclusions

1. Describe what you observed about the soil sample in step 1 of the Procedure section. Was it wet, damp, cohesive, rocky, smelly?

2. What did you observe about the soil in step 2?

3. Describe your observations of the dry soil sample in step 3. Were there any synthetic artifacts? Once-living organisms?

4. How did your descriptions of your soil samples compare to your classmates' descriptions? Were the soil samples different? How so?

 **LAB**

Student Lab: Physical Properties of Soil

How would you describe the color of your soil sample? Is it "brown" or "light brown"? Is your description good enough so that another person could make a comparison?

There are an estimated 1,100 distinguishable soil colors. Soil scientists and geologists use a book of color chips called *The Munsell Soil Color Charts* to describe the color of soil samples. We will use paint panels to match and describe the color of soil samples. Generally, wet soil is darker than dry. We will use dry samples for all the examinations.

Materials

- Dry soil samples
- Stereomicroscope
- Petri dishes
- Color panels
- Magnets
- Plastic bags or food wrap
- UV lamps

Special Safety Considerations

Long-wave UV light sources emit at 366 nm (UVA band). While it may cause eye damage over long exposures, it is still not a good idea to look directly into the light for even a short period of time. Short-wavelength UV light sources, those used for mineral fluorescence, emit at 254 nm (UVC), are extremely hazardous, and can cause loss of vision and cataracts.

Procedure

1. Using a set of color panels, record the color that is the closest match to your soil sample.

2. Draw a magnet covered with a plastic bag or food wrap through your sample. Dislodge any magnetic material and examine it under a stereomicroscope.

90

3. Certain minerals, such as fluorite, some calcites, and willemite, as well as many manufactured articles, such as fibers and plastics, fluoresce. Use the UV light in a darkened area to observe your sample.

Conclusions

1. Which color panel is the closest match to your soil sample?

2. Were you able to dislodge any magnetic material from the soil sample? If so, describe the material.

3. Is there any fluorescence from your soil sample? If so, can you describe what is fluorescing?

Student Lab: Texture of Soil

The particle size of a soil's constituents defines its **texture.** If the samples come from the same source, the range of particle sizes should be very similar.

Materials

- Dry soil sample
- Set of sieves
- Balances

Procedure

1. Arrange the set of sieves in order with the largest holes (the smallest mesh or screen number) on the top and the finest screen at the bottom. Screen numbers of 20, 40, and 100 work well, but the more screens, the better.

2. Weigh between 5 and 10 g of dried soil sample and add to the top sieve. Rub your finger over it to break up any lumps. Put the cover and bottom base on the set of sieves, and shake and tap vigorously for a few minutes.

3. Tap the sides, remove the cover, and weigh the contents of each sieve to the nearest 0.1 g. Record your results in Table 1, including the sieve number. Label and save each fraction of soil for later use.

		\multicolumn{7}{c}{TABLE 1 Soil Texture}						
		\multicolumn{7}{c}{Size Fraction, Sieve No.}						
	Total	+20	+	+	+	+	+	−
Weight, g								
Percent								

Conclusion

1. How best can your data be presented for comparison to the other samples in the class, as well as to a jury?

Student Lab: Density Profile

> ***Density* is defined as mass per unit volume. The ratio of the density of a substance to that of water is called *specific gravity*.**

The particles making up soils vary in density and size. If two soils are from the same location, they should contain particles of similar densities. The density distribution of the particles can be determined by adding soil to a tube containing layers of different-density liquids. Each particle will come to rest at a point in the column that has the same density as that of the particle. A density profile of soil samples may appear as represented in Figure 1. Density gradient columns are prepared by carefully layering various proportions of xylene (d = 0.88 g/cm^3) and bromoform (d = 2.89 g/cm^3).

Materials

- Soil sample
- Density gradient columns
- Balance
- Weighing paper

Special Safety Considerations

Xylene is flammable and slightly toxic. Bromoform is slightly toxic and a **lachrymator** (produces tears).

Procedure

1. For each sample, weigh onto weighing paper 0.1 g of the dried soil fraction that has passed through the 20 mesh screen and remains on the 40 mesh sieve.

2. *Carefully* pour it into a labeled density gradient column. Be careful not to jostle the column. Within hours, the individual particles of the soils will settle to their density levels.

Quartz (SiO$_2$) is a common constituent of many soils. Pure quartz is called silica and has a density of 2.65 g/cm^3, which is very close to the density of bromoform. **Organic** matter, on the other hand, has a density of less than 1.00 g/cm^3.

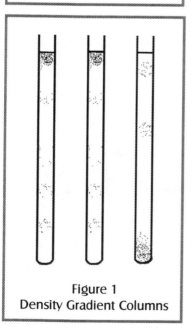

Figure 1
Density Gradient Columns

Conclusions

1. Where would you expect to find sand and compost in a density column?

2. Does the size of the soil particles dictate what level they settle to? Explain.

3. Draw a soil density profile of your sample. Compare it to others and comment on the difference.

93

Student Lab: Chemical Properties of Soil

Soil is a mixture. Some of its constituents may provide information of a chemical nature. Some soils are acidic or basic; those high in limestone ($CaCO_3$), for example, will be basic. Soils containing sulfides (S^{-2}) and sulfates ($SO4^{-2}$) are usually acidic.

Materials

- Soil sample
- Safety goggles
- Soil test kits
- pH paper
- Test tubes
- Beakers
- Distilled water

- Filter paper
- Funnel
- Ammonium hydroxide
- Nitric acid (HNO_3)
- Potassium thiocyanate
- Silver nitrate

Special Safety Consideration

Use caution when handling acid. Even dilute acid can cause chemical burns. Wear goggles.

Procedure

1. Measure the **pH** of the soil by placing a small amount of unseparated sample in a test tube. Add about a centimeter or two of distilled water, shake, let it settle, and then test with pH paper. Compare to the color chart on the pH paper container and record the pH in Table 2.

Testing for nutrients, nitrate, potassium, and phosphate, using a commercial soil or water test kit, can sometimes provide comparative information. Specific chemical tests may identify particular ions that are unique to the soil.

2. Using the soil test kit, follow the procedure for determining nitrate, potassium, and phosphate in your bulk soil sample. Report the results in Table 2.

3. Add about half a gram of the bulk soil sample to a 50-ml beaker. Pour in about 25 ml of 0.5 M nitric acid (HNO_3) and stir gently for a few seconds. Bubbling or frothing indicate the presence of carbonates (limestone).

4. Let the soil settle and filter the mostly clear **supernatant** liquid. Apportion the filtrate to three 10-cm test tubes; about 2 cm in each. Follow the **qualitative** test procedures outlined in steps 5, 6, and 7.

5. Test for iron (Fe^{+3}): Dribble several drops of the thiocyanate solution down the side of the first test tube. A bright red color indicates the presence of iron.

6. Test for chloride (Cl^-): Dribble several drops of silver nitrate solution down the side of the second test tube. A fine, white **precipitate** or milky color indicates the presence of chloride **ion**.

7. Test for copper: Add several drops of dilute ammonia to the third test tube. A deep blue color indicates the presence of dissolved copper.

TABLE 2 Chemical Tests on Soil									
Sample	pH	Color	Carbonate	Nitrogen	Potassium	Phosphate	Iron	Chloride	Copper

Use + to indicate a positive result; − for a negative result.

Forensic Activity: Theft

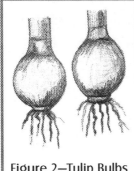

Figure 2—Tulip Bulbs

George and Dianthus Coriopsis, owners of Rara Flora Nurseries, spent years developing a unique black tulip. They had just harvested their first stock crop of approximately 350 2-inch bulbs, which were drying on a screen in their greenhouse. The next day, George went to check on his beauties, and they were gone, except for two or three bulbs on the floor! He estimated their value at about $25,000, as his plan was to copyright them and sell them as stock. He told the police that he suspected a rival in the rare-flower business, Salvia Lobelia of Furtum Flowers, Inc.

The police obtained a search warrant and found several boxes of bulbs that matched the description that George had given them. Mr. Lobelia, however, insisted that they were his and that he had harvested them several days ago from his nursery. He even showed the officers where they had been growing. Samples of soil from Rara Flora Nurseries, from Furtum Flowers, and from the bulbs in question were collected for analysis.

1. Each Investigative Group will receive a package of evidence with three containers of soil. Your job is to determine if there is a match. Prepare a testing protocol and have it approved by your teacher. A Crime Report form must be completed independently by each investigator in each group, with the realization that any one member of the group may be called as an expert witness at trial. Therefore, any conclusions must be justified and able to withstand cross-examination.

2. Which of the samples is the questioned, the unknown?

3. What other forensic evidence might be found to link the suspect to the theft?

4. If charged, will Mr. Lobelia be charged with a misdemeanor or a felony?

96

CRIME REPORT

CASE NO. _____ DATE _____

NATURE OF CRIME _____

DATE OF OCCURENCE _____

TIME OF OCCURENCE _____

LOCATION _____

VICTIM _____

BRIEF HISTORY OF CASE:

TYPE OF EVIDENCE SUBMITTED FOR EXAMINATION _____
List each individual item: use Q for questioned (source unknown);
K for known (source established).

BRIEF DESCRIPTION OF METHODS USED:

CASE NO. _____

RESULTS:

CONCLUSIONS:

SIGNATURE _____ DATE _____

NAME OF INVESTIGATIVE GROUP _____

Teaching Notes and Answer Key

Types of Evidence

Exploration Activities

Materials:
- Paper
- Scissors
- Matchbooks
- 15-cm ruler
- Stereomicroscopes

1. Brand, color, size, model or style, etc.

2. Wear pattern, cuts and blemishes, etc.

3. Ink the sole of the shoe and step on a white piece of paper. Alternatively, the shoe could be photographed or made into a plaster cast.

4. The edge details should be unique.

5. Probably not.

6. Yes, because each detailed tear is different and can be matched to its "twin."

7. No.

8. All straight edges. Individualization might be possible from noting differences in the size of the papers, or if the scissors were nicked and made a distinctive pattern, or if the paper itself showed a pattern or variable characteristics.

9. Yes, see number 8.

10. Probably not, but see number 8.

11. It would be more difficult because of frayed edges.

12. Size, shape, pattern matching, etc.

13. Buy a box of the same kind of paper matchbooks and remove some matches from those that you give to the students.

14. Possible tear pattern, visual comparison especially of the paper, length. Individual, if able to match the match

15. The probability is much lower than in the above exercise when the population was only three.

Forensic Activity: Robbery

Materials:
- Stereomicroscopes
- Tabs from soft-drink cans

1. Are all tabs alike? Do they differ between Coke, Pepsi, Sprite, and other beverages? The problem involves matching the tear patterns and characteristics of many beverage can tabs.

2. From the study described above, a probability can be derived that will affect the strength of the evidence.

Hair Evidence

Exploration Activities

Materials:
- Rulers
- Hand lenses
- Tweezers

Have the students bring in hairs pulled or cut from a pet for later examination.

1. Hair is most likely exchanged in a violent encounter (Locard's principle). Students

should be able to deduce a few properties of hair, such as color and length, that can be used as identifiers.

2. Students should note length, color, and perhaps whether their hair doesn't lie flat, but is wavy or curly. Maybe it is oily, or even has a smell.

Student Lab: Microscopic Examination of Human Hair

Materials:
- Collected hair samples
- Compound microscope
- Microscope slides
- Cover glasses
- Scissors
- Mineral oil or glycerin

2.–3. It is assumed that the school has compound microscopes in biology class. Observation at 30–40× is helpful, but 100× reveals the finer details needed for drawings and comparison to other samples.

4. If you have a microscope with video attachment, projecting a typical hair will allow easy explanation and estimation of the medullary index. Absolute values need not be determined as MI is a ratio.

5. Typical cross sections:

round (straight)　　oval (curly)　　crescent (kinky)
generally Asian　generally Caucasian　　generally
　　　　　　　　　　　　　　　　African-American

6. For a standard diameter, a tool-and-die maker or a metal or machine shop may be able to measure a fine wire or synthetic bristle from a paint brush using a vernier micrometer. An eyepiece reticle to fit your model of microscope can be purchased for $20–30; a stage micrometer for $50–60.

7.–9. Again, a microscope projection is most useful *after* the students have completed their observations. Hair grows at about 1 cm per month. Measure from the root to the change in color.

10. Any difference in characteristics can identify what part of the body hair came from.

11. Students should use the vocabulary in the text to describe the characteristics.

Exploration Activities

1. a. P = 1/30 = 0.033 or the odds of finding such a person in class are 30:1.

   b. P = 8/30 = 0.27

   c. P = 2/30 = 0.27 or 15:1

   d. 2/30 × 630 = 42 boys with black hair

   e. 2/30 + 1/30 = 1/300; 1/33 × 630 = 2.1 girls and boys, but the ratio of girls to boys in class is about 0.5; therefore, there should be one girl with these attributes. We have assumed equal probability of long blond hair between boys and girls, which is not likely but can only be proved by more observations.

2. The answer here depends on the results in Table 2, and the assumption that these characteristics are all independent. Actually, they may not be, since ethnic origins influence several characteristics, which would tend to lower the odds of the hair sample being unique in the population. You may not wish to get into dependent and conditional events as probability gets more complicated.

Let's assume that there are 30 students in your class: 12 with brown hair, seven with hair 3–8 cm long, nine with a fragmented medulla, 12 with hair diameter of

80–100 μm, 10 with a cut (squared) tip, and 28 with no cosmetic treatment. Then, the probability of finding identical hair from two different students is:

$$12/30 \times 7/30 \times 9/30 \times 12/30 \times 10/30 \times 28/30$$
$$= 2{,}540{,}160/729{,}000{,}000 = 0.0035$$

or about 1 in 300. To express this forensically to a jury, one might say: The odds against the hair in question originating from another randomly chosen student are 300 to 1. Or, only 1 out of 300 students would be expected to have these particular hair characteristics. Or, conversely, the probability of identifying the culprit is $1 - 0.0035 = 0.9965$, which is about 300 to 1.

3. Statistically, it is unlikely that there is more than one person with the same six or seven hair characteristics in your class; however, the population is small. The Rule of Large Numbers implies that the actual occurrence approaches the calculated probability as the population increases. Also, it is assumed that the class is diverse. If all the class were Asian, for example, then the odds are going to be quite different.

4. P × number students in school = number of suspects, so if there were 1,200 in the student body, there would be about 4 suspects. You might ask your students the easiest way to identify potential suspects. Obviously, the field can be narrowed based on visual examination of hair color and length. Based on class sampling, how many students would they have to examine further?

5. In class evidence, there are too many similarities to others in the group or population. The more characteristics examined, the greater the probability (odds) of individualizing the evidence. Judges and juries like to know the weight of evidence, and odds are a method of describing that.

Student Lab: Comparison of Animal and Human Hair

Materials:
- Animal hairs
- Human hair
- Compound microscope
- Microscope slides
- Cover glasses
- Mineral oil or glycerin
- Tissues
- Alcohol
- Clear nail polish

Collect various animal hairs from pets, farmers you know, pet hairs brought in by your students, zoos, pet shops, road kill, taxidermists, hunters, furriers, and others with animals. Make several duplicate collections of the common animal hairs. Mount two or three hairs, preferably at least one with an intact tip, on each microscope slide. Fisher's Permount® does a good job as a mounting medium. You may wish to collect good student drawings of animal hairs and make a handout for future reference, such as analysis of the final crime scene.

Forensic Activity: Dognapping

Materials:
- Rulers, tweezers
- Compound microscopes
- Microscope slides
- Cover glasses
- Mineral oil or glycerin
- Alcohol
- Clear nail polish
- Animal hair collection
- Cat hairs
- Gray and/or black dog hairs
- Various human hairs
- Wool fibers

If you divide your class into Investigative Groups (IG), have each group pick a name for themselves and report it on the Crime Report form.

1. Some students may assume that Fred Basset would be a prime suspect, as the motive is obvious. Or there may be a prejudice against bald boxers. The lesson here is "do not make subjective assessments or opinions—they can bias results."

2. Collect appropriate scalp hairs from people. Try to get telogen hairs of the same length from the same person. Prepare a set of evidence envelopes for each investigative group. Avery mailing labels (clear inkjet Label #5160) are useful for both labeling sample envelopes (include also the IG name), and also for use as an evidence seal on the back of the envelope (in red if possible). You may wish to use a Chain of Custody form for authenticity also. Forms are shown in Appendix IV.

George Shepherd is the perpetrator, so put some of his brown hairs in an envelope labeled "QUESTIONED. Hair collected from blanket," etc. Also include several cat hairs, FuFu's, dog hairs, and some wool fibers, which the students should be able to identify and relate to the wool blanket.

A rubric for assessment of the Crime Reports is included in Appendix I for your information.

3. Have the students try it if previous information is lacking. Barring that, one should be able to tell *a* color of a cat since color of other animals' hair is evident.

Fiber Evidence

Exploration Activities

Have the students bring in several samples of fibers from their homes, such as a tuft from a rug, a few threads from clothing, a blanket, or a towel.

1. Silk, wool, mohair, cashmere (goat), angora (goat, rabbit), cotton, linen (flax plant), jute (bark from a plant), sisal (agave plant), hemp (*cannabis* plant), ramie (plant), asbestos, and fiberglass, plus more exotic animal hair, such as llama, alpaca, vicuna, camel, and even yak

2. See Table 2 on page 36.

3. Color, a cotton blend, a tear in the shirt, surface contamination, such as oil or paint or blood

Student Lab: Microscopic Examination of Fibers

Materials:

- Overhead transparency sheets
- Clear 2" sticky tape
- Hand lens or stereomicroscope
- Collection of mounted fiber samples
- Mounting medium
- Compound microscope
- Microscope slides
- Cover glasses
- Mineral oil
- Collection of fabric samples
- Rulers
- Scissors

Use 2-inch clear sticky tape, not the translucent stuff. Make up several permanent standard fiber collections on microscope slides. Fisher Scientific's Permount® is a good mounting medium. Be sure to use fibers that you know are the correct ones. These can be obtained when you acquire the fabric samples you will need later in the chapter, or from sewing thread. It would be helpful if you could include under the same cover glass a sample of undyed and colored fiber. You can buy small such collections from some scientific supply houses; for example, Schoolmasters Science sells a natural textile fibers set for $13. Figure 7 is for reference, but there are variations. Cotton, however, is quite distinctive, and wool should be familiar to those who did the Hair chapter.

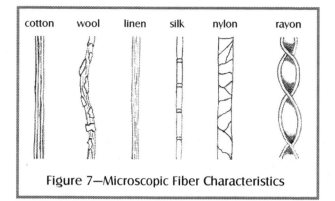

Figure 7—Microscopic Fiber Characteristics

As with the fiber standards, assemble a known fabric collection of 1-inch squares; white (undyed) and colored. If there are blends, define both warp and weft. Wash with soap, not detergent, as you don't want to leave any additives, such as fragrance or optical brighteners. In each activity, give student groups different sets of standards, such as using knowns of different colors or type of weave. This gives students a wider range of observation and experience.

1. Students should note color and such observations as twisted strands, "fuzziness," perhaps surface treatment, etc.

2. They may add diameter, physical characteristics such as number of filaments in a yarn, if it is twisted, etc.

Student Lab: Burning Test

Materials:

- Collection of fabric samples
- Unknown fabric samples
- Tweezers or forceps
- Bunsen burners

Student Lab: Thermal Decomposition

Materials:
- Identified fabric samples
- Unknown fabric samples
- Bunsen burner
- Red and blue litmus paper
- Lead acetate solution
- Filter paper
- Test tubes

Use 13-mm disposable test tubes as the residue is difficult to remove. In place of lead acetate paper, use filter paper wet with 5–10% lead acetate solution.

1. Silk and wool contain sulfur, primarily in the amino acid cystine, in the polypeptide polymer chain. This reacts with the lead's ion from lead acetate to form black precipitate, lead sulphide.

$$Pb^2 + H_2S \longrightarrow PbS + 2H^{++}$$

Student Lab: Chemical Tests

Materials:
- Collection of fabric samples
- Unknown fabric samples
- Hand lenses or stereomicroscopes
- Acetone
- Bleach
- Sodium hydroxide
- Hydrochloric acid
- Sulfuric acid
- 24-well plates
- Stirring rods or toothpicks

Do not use polystyrene well plates because the acetone will dissolve them. 6M NaOH is a 24% solution; 6M HCl can be prepared by diluting concentrated acid 1:1 (be sure to wear safety glasses, work in a well-ventilated place and *always* add acid to water); prepare 6M H_2SO_4 by diluting the concentrated acid 1:2.

1. Such testing can eliminate some samples from consideration, so when coupled with results from other tests, make the identification more conclusive.

Exploration Activity

1. Add samples to water. The one that sinks is polyester. Sometimes, it is necessary to add a small amount of soap to lower the surface tension so no trapped bubbles support the sample.

Student Lab: Examination of Fiber Cross Sections

Materials:
- Top of margarine container
- Duco Cement®
- Sewing needle
- Thread
- Scissors
- Acetone
- Aluminum foil
- Toothpicks
- Compound microscope
- Synthetic fibers
- Razor blade (single edge)
- Mineral oil or glycerin

This should be done carefully, because swiping the diluted cement across the plastic sometimes pulls the embedded fibers out of the hole. Dropping diluted cement prevents this but adds more dried cement, thereby making loss of the fibers more likely when cutting with the razor blade. Fisher's Permount® can also be used; however, it takes a lot longer to dry and it is quite brittle. Use colored samples from a rug; they are easier to see and are probably lobed.

Student Lab: Observing Fluorescence in Fibers

> *Materials:*
> * Fabric samples
> * UV lamp

A simple demonstration of fluorescence involves clear tonic water that fluoresces blue. (See Flinn Scientific Chem-Fax No. 10186.) A more elaborate and colorful demonstration is No. 10218. Black light (ultraviolet light): available from many scientific supply houses or novelty shops. One with only the long wavelength is adequate for this test, but one with both long- and short-wave radiation is more useful in chromatography. The long-wavelength model can be obtained for $10–30. The dual-wavelength model, on which one can select one wavelength or the other, will cost $70–300+. *Caution:* Ultraviolet light can severely damage eyesight. Do not allow anyone to look at it directly.

Student Lab: Dyeing Different Fabrics

> *Materials:*
> * Multifiber ribbon
> * Dyes (Testfabric Stain #1 and #2)
> * Identified fabric samples
> * Unknown fabric sample
> * Acetic acid
> * 50-mL breakers
> * Scissors

Multifiber ribbon and the Testfabric Stains are available from Educational Innovations. One yard costs about $7, so cut it up into 1-cm wide pieces. A package of the two different dyes (stains) costs about $10 for 5 capsules of each color. One dye requires 1 ml of 10% acetic acid.

Use a hair dryer or paper towels to dry the dyed fabrics. Educational Innovations also sells a fabric kit of different fibers for about $18. Be sure the unknown fabric is white and washed with mild soap.

Student Lab: Chromatography of Dyes

> *Materials:*
> * TLC plates or chromatography paper
> * Sodium hydroxide
> * Capillary tubes (open ended)
> * Hot plate
> * Rulers
> * Scissors
> * 250-mL beakers
> * Watchglasses
> * Filter paper
> * Blue fiber samples
> * UV light
> * Iodine crystals
> * Ethyl acetate, ethanol, n-butanol, acetone, ammonium hydroxide

Blue is the most common fiber color. Collect as many different samples of blue cloth, yarn, and thread as you can for your samples. You may wish to try a quick extraction as described to screen out the "no-shows," but check with the UV light first. 0.5M NaOH is a 2% solution.

The TLC sheets (silica gel on plastic or aluminum backing) can be obtained from many scientific supply houses. The plastic back cuts more easily with scissors than the aluminum backed. The sheets are 8" × 8" and rather expensive (for example, Flinn Scientific presently sells one sheet at $13) so cut them up into strips about 1" × 3" (20 per sheet). If you use paper for economy, buy chromatography paper; it doesn't work as well as TLC plates, but it is better than filter paper. Cut the paper strips to 4" in length.

The developing solvent system is ethyl acetate (15 parts by volume); ethanol (7 parts) and water (6 parts). Another effective elution system is n-butyl alcohol (5 parts), acetone (5), water (1), NH_4OH (2). Leftover eluent can be flushed down the drain with plenty of water.

Forensic Activity: Attempted Abduction

Materials:
- Hand lens or stereomicroscope
- Collection of mounted fiber samples
- Mounting medium
- Compound microscopes
- Microscope slides
- Cover glasses
- Mineral oil
- Rulers, scissors
- Tweezers or forceps
- Bunsen burners
- Red and blue litmus paper
- Lead acetate solution
- Filter paper
- Test tubes
- Acetone
- Bleach
- Sodium hydroxide
- Hydrochloric acid
- Sulfuric acid
- 24-well plates
- Stirring rods or toothpicks
- Top of margarine container
- Duco Cement®
- Sewing needle
- Thread
- Aluminum foil

Materials: (continued)
- Razor blade (single edge)
- UV lamp
- TLC plates or chromatography paper
- Capillary tubes
- Hot plates
- 250-mL beakers, watch glasses
- Iodine crystals
- Ethyl acetate, ethanol, n-butanol, acetone, ammonium hydroxide
- Cloth from the van

Emphasize that with trace evidence, sample size is usually limited. Before starting, the student investigative groups should develop an examination protocol. Nondestructive tests should be performed first, and then followed up with those tests that are predicted to give the most unequivocal results. The objective is to obtain the most information from the least amount of material.

A dark; wool, nylon, or polyester; patterned; multicolor cloth will probably work best. Tear it into strips. You may wish to remind the students about blends.

1. See the assessment rubric in Appendix I for suggestions on grading.

2. Matching the tear pattern of the cloth from the van to the strips used on the victim; fingerprints of the victim in the car; fibers from the van's rug on the victim; fibers and hairs of victim on the van's rug.

3. Search a large number of black vans to find the incidence of (1) rags, (2) rags of the same color and pattern used in the crime.

Fiber	Behavior Nearing Flame	Behavior in Flame	Behavior Leaving Flame	Odor	Ash or Residue
			TABLE 3 Burn Test Results		
Cotton	scorches, lights easily	yellow, smoky	continues to burn, glows	burning paper	light gray, feathery ash
Linen	scorches, lights easily	yellow, smoky	continues with afterglow	burning paper	gray, feathery ash
Silk	smolders, then burns	melts and sputters	goes out easily	burning hair	black, shiny beads
Wool	smolders, slow to catch	sizzles as it burns, curls	goes out easily	burning hair	crisp, dark ash
Acetate	fuses away from flame, blackens	lights easily, flickers, melts	continues to burn, small sparks, drips	vinegar, burning wood	black, hard, irregular-shaped beads
Acrylic	fuses, shrinks away	flares, puckers, melts	continues to burn and melt, sputters	acrid, fruity	brittle, hard, black beads
Nylon	fuses, shrinks away	burns slowly, drips, white smoke	dies out	celery	hard, round, grayish beads
Polyester	fuses, shrinks away	burns slowly, melts	burns slowly, sooty smoke	tar	hard, round, black beads
Rayon	scorches, lights easily	burns fast, yellow flame	continues to burn, no glow	burning paper	light gray, feathery ash
Olefin	melts, shrinks away	burns, yellow flame	slowly dies out	wax (pe), diesel fuel (pp)	fused plastic
Fiberglass	coating burns off	no reaction	no reaction	no odor	may fuse solid
Unknown					

TABLE 4 Thermal Decomposition Test Results					
Fiber	Lead Acetate	Red Litmus	Blue Litmus	Residue	Other*
Cotton	no change	no change	no change	light gray ash	
Linen	brown black	no change	turns red	fine gray ash	
Silk	brown black	turns blue	no change	melts and fuses together	
Wool	no change	turns blue	no change	black hollow beads	
Acetate	no change	no change	turns red	irregular black beads	
Acrylic	no change	no change	no change	black gunk	
Nylon	no change	turns blue	no change	stick, hardens to bead	
Polyester	no change	no change	turns red	dark beads	
Rayon	no change	no change	no change	black tar, no ash	
Olefin	no change	no change	no change	black melt	
Fiberglass	no change	no change	no change	no change	
Unknown					

* "Other" may be used to note type of smoke or other observations

TABLE 5 Chemical Test Results					
Fiber	Acetone	Bleach	NaOH	HCl	H_2SO_4
Cotton	no change	no change	no change	no change	no change
Linen	no change	no change	no change	no change	no change
Silk	no change	no change	no change	no change	no change
Wool	no change	no change	yellow disintegrates	no change	no change
Acetate	translucent disintegrates	no change	no change	no change	no change
Acrylic	no change	no change	may yellow	no change	no change
Nylon	no change	no change	no change	shrivels up	disintegrates white ppt
Polyester	no change	no change	no change	no change	no change
Rayon	no change	no change	no change	no change	no change
Olefin	no change	no change	no change	no change	no change
Fiberglass	no change	no change	no change	no change	no change
Unknown					

Blood Evidence

Exploration Activities

1. $0.04 \times 0.15 = 0.006$ or 1 out of 167 people.

2. $0.10 \times 0.27 \times 0.15 = 0.0041$ or 1 out of 250. This is pretty strong evidence, but it depends on the circumstances that control the number of suspects (population).

3. One-twelfth of average adult weight. The density of blood is about that of water, so it works out that dividing your weight by 12 gives the number of pints of blood in your body.

No human blood products are used in any activities described.

Student lab: Detection of Blood

Place a few drops or smudges of some or all of the following substances each on a 1" x 1" piece of white cotton cloth:

- red food coloring or fake blood
- ferric nitrate
- ketchup
- dark red or brown paint
- red magic marker
- tea and/or coffee
- rust
- cherry furniture stain
- dirt
- animal blood

Blood can be obtained from a friendly veterinarian or simply from raw beef or liver. Code each sample and be sure they are dry before distributing to the class. You may wish to have each investigative group perform blood tests on all the stained samples or on different stains, but always include the blood.

Hematest® tablets or Hemastix® strips are Bayer products used for determining occult blood in urine. The active chemical is a benzidine derivative, allegedly a carcinogen, but perfectly harmless under the circumstances of use. Available at a good pharmacy or on the Internet. They are expensive (100 tabs of Hematest™ are presently about $50; 50 strips of Hemastix™ are about $25), so subdivide them for each test. In the quantity used, this material can be flushed down the drain.

Kastle-Meyer reagent: Dissolve 1–2 g phenolphthalein in 100 ml 25% KOH solution. Boil with 1g zinc dust until colorless. Decant. Dilute with ethanol to 1 liter. Be sure the zinc is dry before discarding, as the dust is pyrophoric.

Luminol solution: Dissolve 0.1 g luminol and 0.5 g Na_2CO_3 in 100 ml of water. Add 0.7 g sodium perborate just before use. The final solution has a limited shelf life. Both reagents are available from Flinn Scientific. A spray bottle with a fine mist works well.

The luminol spiral is a neat teacher demonstration of thermoluminescence. Make up two solutions, each in a 500-ml flask:

Solution A
    2.0 g sodium carbonate
    0.1 g luminol
    12 g sodium bicarbonate
    0.25 g ammonium carbonate monohydrate
    0.2 g cupric sulfate pentahydrate
    475 ml distilled water

Solution B
    30 ml 3% hydrogen peroxide
    475 ml distilled water

The luminol spiral is made of Tygon tubing, 5–6 clamps, a ring stand, and a 2-liter flask or other receptacle for waste. Assemble it as in the diagram.

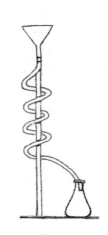

Dim the lights and slowly pour the solutions simultaneously into the funnel. A bright blue glow will be observed. The product may be disposed of down the sink in these quantities.

A spectacular demonstration of luminol detection is to use a colored T-shirt or fabric that has been obviously stained with a nonblood material and also animal blood. Cut it in half and wash one piece. Take it into a darkened room, wail until your audience has become accustomed to the dark, and spray with luminol. (A bloody handprint is really awesome!)

1. Presumptive or screening tests presume the presence of the substance but are not confirmatory. For example, a positive Hematest™ may also be caused by hypochlorite bleach. A negative test, however, verifies the absence of the substance under test.

Student Lab: Testing Human or Animal Blood

Materials:
- Sodium silicate
- Food coloring
- Hydrochloric acid
- Test tube
- Pipets

Simulated Precipitin Test: For the human antiserum, dilute sodium silicate with water and a drop or two of yellow food coloring. Sodium silicate solution can be obtained, for example, from Flinn. The dilute blood sample is merely 1M HCl colored very light red. Experiment until you get the desired white coagulation at the interface of the two liquids.

1. Is it blood? Is it human blood? How did it get there?

Forensic Activity: Assault

Materials:
- Corn syrup
- Food coloring
- Calcium nitrate
- Sodium carbonate
- Magnesium sulfate
- Stereomicroscope
- Microscope slides
- Pipets or dropping bottles
- Toothpicks

Make up a quart or more of simulated blood, as you will need a lot for the blood spatter for this part of the chapter. Add to clear corn syrup a drop or more of red food coloring and then a little blue coloring to deepen the red. You won't need much simulated blood and sera for the typecasting activity, but make up enough for your ultimate crime scene also.

- Simulated anti-A and anti-Rh sera: Dissolve 16g of $Ca(NO_3)_2$ in 100 ml of water, color yellow with food dye. Divide in half for each serum.

- Simulated anti-B serum: Dissolve 5 g Na_2CO_3 in 50 ml water, color yellow with food dye.

- Simulated blood for suspects 1 and 7 (Type A+): Dissolve 5 g Na_2CO_3 in 10 ml water, add to 50 ml of the simulated blood and stir.

- Simulated blood for suspects 2 and 5 (Type B–): Dissolve 9 g $Ca(NO_3)_2$ in 10 ml water, add to 50 ml of the simulated blood and stir.

- Simulated blood for suspects 3 and 6 (Type AB+): Dissolve 7 g $Mg(SO_4)_2$ in 10 ml water, add to 50 ml of the simulated blood and stir.

- Simulated blood for suspects 4 and 8 (Type O–): Add 10 ml water to 50 ml of the simulated blood and stir.

- Simulated blood from the crime scene: AB+

The $MgCO_3$ reaction is more of a coagulation with slight cloudiness, whereas the precipitates of $Ca(CO_3)_2$ and $CaSO_4$ show a distinct cloudiness. Adding too much serum dilutes the "blood drop" and obscures the coagulation and cloudiness. To be correct, controls should be run; that is, known blood samples are analyzed and results compared to those of the suspects.

A number of scientific supply houses sell ABO/Rh typing kits/labs. For example, Wards offers several kinds.

Rather than using a stereomicroscope, a good magnifying glass is quite adequate. Place each drop of blood on the microscope slide; placing it over an X on white paper beneath allows observation of developing cloudiness.

The simulated blood never really dries but just gets stickier. Soap and water clean it up quite easily.

1. Two suspects can be linked to the assault: 3 and 6.

Suspect #	Name	Anti-A	Anti-B	Anti-Rh	Bloodtype
1	Angus McIntosh	+	−	+	A+
2	Arthur Redwell	−	+	−	B−
3	Robert Braeburn	+	+	+	AB+
4	Jonathan Gold	−	−	−	O−
5	Phillip Macoun	−	+	−	B−
6	Baldwin Sapp	+	+	+	AB+
7	Mortimer Gravenstein	+	−	+	A+
8	Jimmy Jon Gala	−	−	−	O−
9	Crime Scene	+	+	+	AB+

2. Suspect 8

3. $0.45 \times 0.85 = 0.382$ or 38.2% of the population

4. Type AB

5. Type O, because it has no antigens to react with antibodies

6. Type AB because it has no antibodies to react with A or B antigens

7. Types B and O

8. Yes if it still retains *all* its factors, but DNA typing is easier and can also give unequivocal results.

Student Lab: Blood Pattern Analysis

Materials:

- 3–4' freezer, butcher, or kraft paper (in a pinch)
- Masking tape
- Simulated blood. Add water to the basic recipe to achieve the desired viscosity.
- Dishwasher detergent
- Pipets or eye droppers
- Paper, protractor, meter stick, ruler, string
- Syringe, plastic knife or similar object
- Trig table (Appendix) or trig function calculator

This activity is inquiry based, thus little information is provided to the student. The material provided to the teacher can be used to guide the class through the steps required to answer the questions posed.

The teacher may wish to lead a discussion on the type of information that can be gleaned from the study of blood patterns. For example: type of weapon used; how many gunshots, stabs, or blows were inflicted; sequence of injuries; position of the victim and assailant; if they were moving during the attack; whether the assailant was right or left handed; the degree of force used by the perpetrator; whether there might be blood on the assailant; or if the victim was moved after the attack. This is a good place to show at least the bloodstain portions of "The Killer's Trail," a 60-minute NOVA videotape of the Sheppard case.

A roll of freezer, butcher, or kraft paper spread out and taped to the floor and walls of the working area will allow protection and potentially provide cutout samples of the stains.

Use the basic synthetic blood substitute, but add 1 tbsp (15 ml) dishwasher detergent to each quart (or liter) to allow easy clean up. The drops will not dry but will remain sticky.

A digital camera can be used very effectively to record information.

Height: Student investigation teams should use a beral or Pasteur pipet to drop blood substitute vertically from different heights onto a smooth paper surface. They should describe the shape of the drop and its size, and note relationships and trends. Perhaps the fastest group could investigate drop shape as a function of surface texture.

Velocity: The density of blood is 1.06 g/cm^3 and its viscosity is 6 times that of water. It's average drop size as a result of surface tension and viscosity is 0.05 ml for free fall. As with all objects in freefall, a drop of blood accelerates 32 ft/sec^2 (9.8 m/sec^2). Any object will fall at this rate until it reaches its terminal velocity, which is a direct function of drop size. For the average drop size, the terminal velocity of 25 ft/sec is reached after a fall of 4 feet, so drop size should not change above that. The majority of high-velocity droplets, which tend to be less than 1 mm, will usually travel no more than 46 inches in a horizontal direction.

Angle of Impact: The students should use white paper on cardboard and prop it up at an angle. Then, using a pipet, direct a drop of blood onto the paper from a fixed height. They should record the shape of the drop as a function of the angle of impact, as measured with a protractor. It is important that they note that the length to width ratio increases with decreasing impact angle.

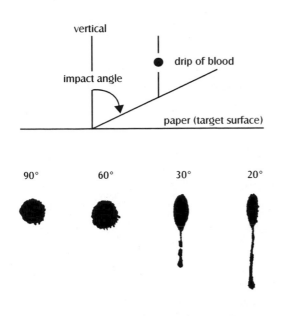

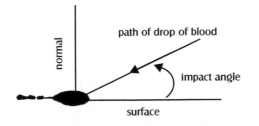

Direction of Travel: From the previous activity, the students should realize that the distorted end of the drop of blood points in the direction of travel. To emphasize this point, have the students fling drops of blood off a stirring rod or finger and note the shape of the stain relative to the direction of travel.

The drop shape relationship observed in the previous activity can be described trigonometrically by the following relationship:

$$\text{impact angle, } I = \text{arc sin} \frac{\text{drop width, w}}{\text{drop length, l}}$$

Arc sin can be calculated with a hand-held

calculator or found in a table such as that in Appendix IV.

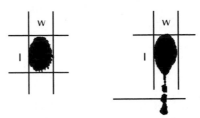

Have students prepare a table like the one below, using their results from the previous activity.

		impact angle, °	
width, w	length, l	calculated	measured

Origin of Blood Source: If there are multiple drops of blood, then their origin can be located by triangulation.

Have students fling drops of blood from a fixed location. Stretch string through the long axis of each well-formed drop and locate the area of convergence.

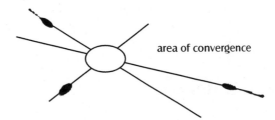

Next, place a ring stand or some standing unit on the area of convergence. Then determine angle of impact for each drop. Using string, masking tape, and a protractor, raise the string to the calculated angle and attach to the ring stand. Convergence indicates location of point of origin of the blood.

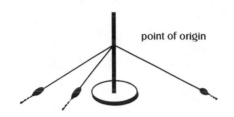

point of origin

Left or Right Handed: Have a right-handed student stand near a wall covered with paper and dip a plastic knife, tongue depressor, or other similar object in a container of simulated blood, then rapidly pull back the arm. The spattered blood follows an arc with the tail of each drop pointing up for an overhead thrust.

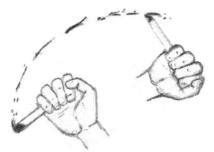

Now, have a left-handed student do it. How is the cast-off pattern different? Is it important to know where the victim was? Have students predict the pattern resulting from multiple stabs, and then try it.

Glass Evidence

Student Lab: Macroscopic and Microscopic Examination of Glass Pieces

Materials:
- Glass samples of different sizes
- UV light
- Stereomicroscope
- Ruler

1. Aside from the obvious, students may be able to identify fiber optics, ceramics, beads

for reflecting signs, fiberglass, etc. as uses for glass.

The teacher should assemble sets of 1–3 cm pieces of various glass samples, such as:

- Bottle—clear, brown, green
- Glass or tumbler
- Light bulb—clear, frosted
- Window pane
- Leaded glass ("crystal")
- Glass from a TV or computer monitor
- Eyeglass lens
- Ovenware, such as Pyrex®
- Auto glass, from front window and side window. The front windshield of an automobile is laminated with plastic sandwiched between two layers of window glass. The side windows are made of tempered (heat-treated) glass that does not shatter but breaks into small squares.
- Headlight glass
- Fiberglass
- Fiber-optic glass
- Ceramics
- Quartz
- Uranium glass

Body shops, garage sales, or a local college or university if they have a glassblowing shop are all willing sources. Make several sets of each macrosample in labeled containers (empty film canisters work very well). Smash up a portion of each sample to make 2-mm or smaller fragments and make several sets of these in the same way. These can be used to prepare samples for the lab. You may wish to show the students a few of the fragmented samples to compare with the larger portion to see if they can match them.

For small, thin fragments of glass, use labeled fragments prepared from the larger samples.

See Student Lab: Observing Fluorescence in Fibers for information about UV lights.

2. Most glasses do not fluoresce. Exceptions are uranium glass, which fluoresces bright yellow; lead glass ("crystal"), a dull white; and some quartz glasses that slightly fluoresce a violet color.

3. Color, thickness, opacity, curvature, surface features, fluorescence.

5. A good millimeter ruler is adequate.

Student Lab: Measuring the Density of a Glass Fragment

See Student Lab: Density Profile in the Soil Evidence chapter for sources and care of bromoform. Bromobenzene is also available from Aldrich or Flinn. It is moderately toxic and possibly irritating to skin. The mixture of these products can be disposed of by evaporation.

1. Glass is less dense than bromoform.

3. This is a trick question because we are dealing with density, weight (mass) per unit volume, not weight *per se*. So if another sample is denser than the first, it will sink. Adding additional drops of bromoform to "float" it will allow calculation of its density.

Student Lab: Determining Refractive Index

> *Demo Materials:*
> - Pyrex rod
> - Beakers
> - Glycerine
> - Ghost Crystals

The teacher can demonstrate refractive index by immersing a pyrex rod in a beaker of glycerin. The refractive indices are both 1.47 (be careful—that of glycerin will change with temperature). Another demonstration involves Flinn Scientific's Ghost Crystals. These polymers absorb water to the extent that they become

invisible in water; thus, they have the same index of refraction as water.

Refraction can be demonstrated easily by immersing a glass rod in a beaker of water. When viewed obliquely above the surface of the water, the rod appears to bend. Looking at it through the beaker, it appears the rod is broken (offset) at the surface of the water. This results from the curvature of the glass. Ask the students to predict which way the rod will appear to bend when $n_{rod} \ll n_{water}$.

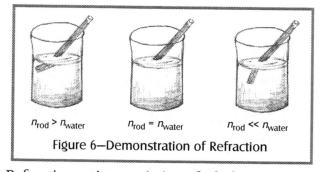

$n_{rod} > n_{water}$ $n_{rod} = n_{water}$ $n_{rod} \ll n_{water}$

Figure 6—Demonstration of Refraction

Refractive optics consisting of a light source include: a ray box, a set of prisms, some pieces of glass and plastic with one smooth polished straight edge, a glass water bath with one clear straight edge. This type of material can be purchased from Flinn Scientific or Arbor Scientific, for example. Cost can run from $100 and up.

Clean out your kitchen cabinet for different test substances. Other substances might include rubbing alcohol (isopropanol), salt solutions of different concentrations, mineral oil, and so on.

> *Materials:*
> - Demo materials
> - Optics kit
> - Protractor
> - Sine table
> - Oils, chemicals
> - Salt
> - CRC *Handbook of Chemistry and Physics*

1. To keep things simple when students measure the angle of incidence and angle of refraction, they need not trace the exit beam.

2. Velocity is different in different media. See the definition.

3. Compare the refractive indices from Table 3. Water has the lower value, so it will bend light less than glass.

4. Any clear material with $n \neq n_{water}$

5.–6. A list of refractive indices can be found in the CRC *Handbook of Chemistry and Physics*. Differences can be explained by measurement errors, temperature effects, contaminants, mixtures, and other causes.

Student Lab: Determining Refractive Index of Glass Fragments

Materials:
- Glass fragments
- Hand lens
- Alcohol
- Beakers
- Watch glasses
- Forceps or tweezers
- Refractive index liquids

To set this experiment up so that it is least frustrating to the students, select glass fragment samples that are different enough to differentiate with the refractive index liquids available. You can mix the oils proportionately to obtain the proper refractive index for each sample. Set up one or more stations by placing a few milliliters of each liquid in a watch glass on white paper. Label each with the refractive index. Provide a small beaker of alcohol for rinsing the forceps and sample upon removal, and a paper towel for blotting the sample to prevent contamination. Be sure students immerse the glass fragments completely and clean them well between immersions.

Refractive index liquids: olive oil (light, refined) from a grocery store; castor oil from a drug store. Clove oil is also called eugenol. It may be available from a gourmet kitchen shop, but the product may be diluted with alcohol. Flinn sells this as well as other oils. It is generally less expensive to buy it from Aldrich.

1. The first RI has a frequency of about 9; the second, about 20. The latter RI is 20/9 or about twice as common; therefore, it has about half the evidentiary value.

Forensic Activity: Burglary

Materials:
- Headlight glass fragments
- Window glass fragments
- UV lights
- Stereomicroscope
- Rulers
- Bromoform, bromobenzene
- Beral or Pasteur pipets
- Tweezers
- Test tubes with rack
- Stirring rods
- Hand lens
- Alcohol
- Beakers
- Watch glasses
- Refractive index liquids

The RI measurement is not as sensitive or precise as density, so it is important to have two different densities. Translucent orange pill containers are good to use for evidence. You can dress them up with a nice evidence label and seal. Isoprophyl alcohol works well to remove any adhering adhesive.

1. See the rubric in Appendix I.

2. The evidence only indicates that the suspect was at the scene of the crime during or after the burglary. It is circumstantial evidence. But, if the suspect denied ever having been in the house, then the evidence becomes much stronger.

3. Blood on the glass, footprints outside in the dirt and inside of dirt, fingerprints (especially on the doorknob), soil on the suspect's sneakers, stolen property

Exploration Activities

1. The pattern on the left was made first.

2. See Figure 4.

Student Lab: Analysis of Glass Fracture Patterns

Bullet holes in glass: Shoot at an inexpensive glassed picture frame at least twice with a .22 or BB gun, or even a slingshot using a small ball bearing. Pull one piece of glass out to view stress cracks. Use masking tape to protect all sides except the one showing stress cracks. Tape the front of the picture-frame glass with clear tape. Try shooting a thin sheet of plastic also.

Soil Evidence

Student Lab: Examination of Soil

Materials:
- Wet soil sample
- Dry soil sample
- Notebook paper
- Stereomicroscope
- Petri dishes
- Drying oven

Have the students bring in 2–4 oz of soil from one location around their home (a handful of soil is about 3 oz, 100 g). Take half and dry it at 80–100°C overnight. Be sure both samples are labeled.

Student Lab: Physical Properties of Soil

Materials:
- Dry soil samples
- Stereomicroscope
- Petri dishes
- Color panels
- Magnets
- Plastic bags or food wrap
- UV lamp(s)

Get sets of tans and browns from your local paint store—enough for every group. Munsell Soil Color Charts cost over $100.

A cow magnet works well, but any strong magnet will do. Opaque, angular grains are probably the mineral magnetite. Small opaque, spherical particles may be micrometeorites.

Black light (ultraviolet light): available from any scientific supply house or rock shop. One with only the long wavelength is adequate and considerably cheaper; expect to pay approximately $25. *Caution:* Ultraviolet light can severely damage eyesight. Do not allow anyone to look at it directly.

Student Lab: Texture of Soil

Materials:
- Dry soil sample
- Sets of sieves
- Balances

In order to save time and keep costs at a minimum, have each Investigative Group pick one sample for each test henceforth.

A good set of brass sieves is very expensive. A small plastic set of sieves: 20, 40, and 100 mesh are most suitable, small size is preferable (2–4");

available, for example, from Carolina Biological Supply. It is very important for reproducible results to thoroughly shake and tap.

1. A bar graph has the most impact and is easiest to compare. But have the students use a computer spreadsheet to come up with a scheme.

Student Lab: Density Profile

Materials:
- Soil sample
- Density gradient columns
- Column stand
- Balance
- Weighing paper
- Bromoform
- Xylene
- Parafilm

The density gradient columns are constructed from 10-mm glass tubing, 30 cm long, with one end sealed. If you have a college or university nearby, ask if they have a scientific glassblower. They are usually happy to help out local schools. Or make it yourself with a Meeker burner—it takes a little practice, but it doesn't have to be beautiful. Be sure to use Pyrex® glass and anneal it (cool it gradually in the flame by diminishing the flow of air). A 2 × 4 piece of wood, with the appropriate-size holes drilled in it makes a good stand.

Various proportions of xylene ($d = 0.88$ g/cm^3) and bromoform ($d = 2.89$ g/cm^3) are mixed and layered in the column with the pure bromoform on the bottom and the pure xylene on the top. Make up mixtures according to the table below, which will fill one or two tubes.

ml, liquid	
Bromoform	Xylene
3.0	0
2.5	0.5
2.0	1.0
1.5	1.5
1.0	2.0
0.5	2.5
0	3.0

Pour each gently down the side of the column, cover with parafilm or a cork (not aluminum foil), and let it sit overnight to equilibrate. Be careful not to jar or wiggle it.

Xylene and bromoform can be purchased through ordinary chemical supply houses. Bromoform over time will darken as it releases bromine, even in its brown glass bottle. Since it is so expensive, it is worth cleaning by merely filtering it through activated charcoal.

Caution: The liquids used to make up the density gradient columns are toxic. Make up the columns in a hood or well-ventilated spot and leave them there. (This would be a work station where each IG of students adds one particular sample to one tube). Wash your hands if you get any liquid on them. After the experiment, place the contents in a shallow, open, labeled container and let evaporate to dryness in a hood.

1. Sand on the bottom, organic matter floating on the top. Dark iron-rich minerals are generally heavier than quartz.

2. No, only the time it takes to get there. Density is the ratio g/cm^3.

Student Lab: Chemical Properties of Soil

Materials:
- Soil sample
- Safety goggles
- Soil test kits
- pH paper
- Test tubes
- Beakers
- Distilled water
- Filter, filter paper
- Acetic acid
- Funnel
- Ammonium hydroxide
- Ammonium oxalate
- Barium hydroxide
- Nitric acid
- Potassium chromate
- Potassium thiocyanate
- Silver nitrate
- Sodium sulfide

Soil test kits can be found in stores that sell gardening supplies or from scientific supply houses. They usually measure nitrogen, phosphorus, potassium (potash), and pH. You can scale back and divide the tablet or capsule to get more tests for the buck. Carolina Biological Supply sells an NPK Soil Test Kit (CE-18-1875) allowing 50 tests; Forestry Suppliers also sells this for about the same price (#77960).

Caution: Concentrated acetic acid is a flammable liquid and is corrosive; concentrated ammonium hydroxide is severely corrosive and a respiratory hazard. Work in a hood or well-ventilated area when making up solutions. Silver nitrate and potassium chromate are corrosive solids that can cause burns and will stain skin. See Flinn Scientific catalog for safety information.

Specific chemical test strips are available from Fisher Scientific as EM Quant Test Strips, but they are rather expensive. Use 0.1 M solutions of the test solutions of potassium thiocyanate (KSCN) and silver nitrate ($AgNO_3$). One M ammonium hydroxide (NH_4OH) is adequate for the copper test. Use 13×100-mm disposable test tubes, 50–100-ml beakers, #1 filter paper.

You may wish to add more tests. Ammonium oxalate (0.1 M) will produce a white precipitate with Ca^{+2}, as does 0.1 M barium hydroxide with $SO4^{-2}$. Many heavy-metal sulfides are black; zinc sulfide, however, is white, may be slightly yellow, and is formed by the addition of 0.1 M Na_2S. Soluble lead can be detected by shaking a sample of soil in water, not acid, adding a little acetic acid to the filtrate and then, 0.1 M K_2CrO_4. A yellow precipitate indicates lead. Test strips for lead in soil can be purchased from some lab suppliers, but they are costly and have limited shelf life. The small amounts of waste material generated can safely be flushed down the drain.

Forensic Activity: Theft

Materials:
- Stereomicroscope
- Petri dish
- Drying oven
- Color panels
- Magnets
- Plastic bags
- UV lamp(s)
- Sets of sieves
- Balances
- Density gradient columns
- Column stand
- Weighing paper
- Bromoform
- Xylene
- Parafilm
- Safety goggles
- Soil test kits

(continued)

Materials (continued):
- pH paper
- Test tubes
- Beakers
- Filter, filter paper
- Acetic acid
- Ammonium hydroxide
- Ammonium oxalate
- Barium hydroxide
- Nitric acid
- Potassium chromate
- Potassium thiocyanate
- Silver nitrate
- Sodium sulfide
- Potting soil, sand

Use garden soil or potting soil. Add some sand and/or regular soil to one sample to make it different. To make this exercise easy, you may wish to add a few fertilizer pellets, those little round beads, to one sample, or spike two with one of the nutrients or a chemical that had been analyzed.

1. See the assessment rubric in Appendix I for suggestions on grading.

2. The soil from the bulbs is the questioned material, since the origin is not yet clear.

3. Tire tracks or footprints at the scene of the crime

4. Misdemeanor (See chapter on Forensic Background.)

Rubrics: Assessing Laboratory Reports

This book contains several student laboratory assignments for which you will produce a written report. Lab reports are important because they are a written recipe for another scientist to replicate your findings. Information should include:

- *Purpose:* Why is this lab being performed? What is the objective of the lab?

- *Hypothesis:* Given the initial level of knowledge, what do you expect to find out at the end?

- *Materials list:* A well-organized materials list makes it easier for anyone trying to replicate your results to understand what was done.

- *Procedure:* Even though a procedure is suggested in the lab write-ups, you should include the procedure you actually followed.

- *Data:* What actually took place in the lab?

- *Conclusion:* What were the results? Did your hypothesis match the data? If something went wrong, what do you think happened?

In order to give teachers and parents a quick guide to assessing lab reports, we have constructed the following rubric:

	1	2	3	4
Understanding of concept	poor	adequate	good	outstanding
Methodology	poor	adequate	good	outstanding
Organization of experiment	poor	adequate	good	outstanding
Organization of report	poor	adequate	good	outstanding

Rubrics: Assessing Crime Reports

Topic	Score	Score × 1.00	Score × 0.85	Score × 0.70	Score × 0.50
Appearance	5	Neat, complete	Complete	Some omissions	Many omissions, mess, difficult to read
Organization	15	Well-organized, logical (table)	Organized	Poorly organized, rambling	Difficult to follow and to find information
Content:					
1st five lines	5	Detailed with correct date and time estimates	Complete	Incomplete, general	Incomplete, wrong, or no date, time
History	5	Brief and clear summary abstracted from text	Summary	Not brief, omissions	Inaccurate, incomplete
Evidence	10	Orderly list with Q, K designations; e.g., "K, Shepherd, hair from . . ."	List complete without details	Omits Q, K	Incomplete information
Methods	15	Brief description; e.g., macro and microscopic exam of color, etc. Q *compared* to K	Not as much detail	Does not list all characteristics examined, no mention of comparing	Difficult to understand method or observations
Results	45	Like Table 1 in text, characteristics vs. sample; e.g., incl. FuFu and Q, recognizes wool, highlights K and Q matches	Table or logical display	Incomplete or difficult to review results	Incomplete, cannot find relationships, faulty interpretation

Rubrics: Assessing Essays

In addition to lab reports, you will also be assigned several essays. In addition to using material provided in this book, you should explore other sources by doing outside research on the subject matter.

In order to give parents and teachers a quick guide to assessing topic-driven essays, we have constructed the following rubric:

	1	2	3	4
Quality of research	poor	adequate	good	outstanding
Organization of material	poor	adequate	good	outstanding
Presentation of material	poor	adequate	good	outstanding
Spelling, grammar, and style	poor	adequate	good	outstanding

Resources

Types of Evidence

Internet sites:

Testimonial Evidence:
www.crimeandclues.com/testimony.htm

Statistics as Applied to Fiber Evidence:
www.fbi.gov/hq/lab/fsc/backissu/oct1999/houck.htm

Probability:
http://chemistry.about.com/gi/dynamic/offsite.htm?site=http%3A%2F%2Fwww.math.uah.edu%2Fstat%2F

Probability of Independent Events:
www.mathgoodies.com/lessons/vol6/independent_events.html

Probability Theory Applied to Forensics:
www.cpes.sussex.ac.uk/fslp/lnotes/probability.pdf

Hair Evidence

See also Saferstein, Evans, and others in the General References.

Internet sites for famous cases:

www.crimelibrary.com/serial_killers/predators/williams/index_1.html?sect=21
Atlanta child murders; lengthy account of the Wayne Williams case

www.crimelibrary.com/criminal_mind/forensics/trace/4.html?sect=21
"Caught by a Hair," Telluride, CO case

Internet sites for general hair information:

www.wcsscience.com/hair/page.html
Short piece on hair including animal with some good photos of human hair cuticle and tips

www.crimelibrary.com/criminal_mind/forensics/trace/5.html?sect=21
Forensic hair evidence analysis

www.nida.nih.gov/pdf/monographs/monograph167/146-160_Miller.pdf
FBI treatise on history, results, etc. of testing hair for drugs

Video, *Beaten by a Hair: Ultraviolet Microscopy,* #CBA 8606. Films for the Humanities & Science, P. O. Box 2053, Princeton, NJ, 08543-2053; www.films.com (1999). $129.

Fiber Evidence

Fisher, David. *Hard Evidence.* New York: Dell, 1995

"Industries, Textile" *The New Encyclopedia Britannica,* vol 21, Macropedia, 15th edit., 1993.

Internet sites for fiber forensics and famous cases:

www.crimelibrary.com/serial_killers/notorious/index.html
Lengthy account of the Wayne Williams case

www.fbi.gov/hq/lab/fsc/backissu/april1999/houckch1.htm
"Introduction to Forensic Fiber Examination"

www.fbi.gov/hq/lab/fsc/backissu/april1999/
houckch2.htm
"Microscopy of Textile Fibers"

www.fbi.gov/hq/lab/fsc/backissu/april1999/
houckch4.htm
"Thin-Layer Chromatography of Nonreactive Dyes in Textile Fibers"

www.fbi.gov/hq/lab/fsc/backissu/april1999/
houckch7.htm
"Fabrics and Cordage"

Internet sites for general fiber, fabric, and polymer information:

http://plc.cwru.edu/tutorial/enhanced/
main.htm
Awesome, interactive college-level site on polymerization, and optical properties of polymers such as birefringence, etc.

www.fabrics.net
Short definitions of natural and synthetic fibers and their fabric properties

www.cem.msu.edu/~reusch/VirtualText/
polymers.htm#polmr1
Good introductory college-level treatise on polymers

www.vectranfiber.com/index1.html
A very complete dictionary of fiber technology

www.extension.umn.edu/
topics.html?topic=6&subtopic=13
List of how to clean different stains off fabrics—very handy

Manufactured Fiber Fact Book, Education Department, American Fiber Manufacturers Assoc., Inc., Suite 310, 1150 17th St., NW, Washington, DC, 20036, 1988.

Meloan, C. E., "Fibers, Natural and Synthetic," *Chemistry,* 51 (April 1978).

"The Common Thread: Multiple Forensics," video, Films for the Humanities & Sciences, P.O. Box 2053, Princeton, NJ 08543-2053. www.films.com

Wood, Clair G., "Natural Dyes," *ChemMatters,* December 1986, p. 4-7. American Chemical Society.

See also Saferstein, Evans, and others in the General References.

Blood Evidence

"Blood," *Kids Discover,* 9, (4, April 1999). www.kidsdiscover.com

Gottfried, Sandra and Maria Sedotti, "Blood Markers," Mystery Matters in *Chem Matters,* pp 4–6, April 1992. American Chemical Society.

Internet Sites:

http://faculty.ncwc.edu/toconnor/425/
425lect13.htm
Forensic serology

http://brazoria-county.com/sheriff/id/
blood/index.htm
Good overview of blood spatter and terminology

http://brazoria-county.com/sheriff/id/
blood/index.htm
Technical description of some real cases with blood patterns

www.physics.carleton.ca/~carter
Computerized blood-spatter analysis

www.crimeandclues.com
Good site for photos of blood spatter, etc.

"The House that Roared," Forensic Files, Court TV, January 11, 2001. Available from Films for the Humanities & Sciences, 24 min for $129 (www.films.com; 800-257-5126). Use of luminol

"The Killer's Trail," videotape of the Sam Sheppard murder case with blood-spatter evidence. Available from http://main.wgbh.org/wgbh/shop/products/wg2613.html for $19.95.

See also Saferstein, Evans, and others in the General References.

Glass Evidence

Fisher, David. *Hard Evidence*. New York: Dell, 1995.

Handbook of Chemistry and Physics. Boca Raton: CRC Press LLC, any edition.

Internet sources:

www.channel4.co.uk/science/microsites/S/science/society/forensic_trace.html
Good overview with diagrams of glass evidence

www.gwu.edu/~forchem/OurMainPage/mainpage.htm
Technical aspects of RI determination of glass

www.britannica.com. Search for "glass"

Miller, Hugh, *What the Corpse Revealed; Murder and the Science of Forensic Detection*, St. Martin's (1999). Available at Amazon for $6.99. Chapter 4; "Vendetta" describes how a determined investigator puts the pieces of a bottle back together to catch a killer, with a surprise ending!

See also Saferstein, Evans, and others in the General References.

Soil Evidence

Frazier, Jane Justus, "Sand Studies," *The Science Teacher"* May 1996, 14. Laboratory experiment.

Internet sites of famous cases:

www.interpol.int/Public/Forensic/IFSS/meeting13/Reviews/Soil.pdf
Summary of techniques used in the forensic exam of soils, with some cases

http://web.umr.edu/~rogersda/forensic_geology/ Forensic%20Geology.doc
Cases from Murray's "Forensic Geology"

http://web.umr.edu/~rogersda/forensic_geology
Cases including the famous "How geologists unraveled the mystery of Japanese vengeance bombs in World War II"

http://mccoy.lib.siu.edu/projects/geology/geol483/int483_b.html
Brief summary of four cases

http://mccoy.lib.siu.edu/projects/geology/geol483/ralston.html
Recounting a famous case

www.si.edu/opa/researchreports/9582/9582mnrl.htm
Webb, Jo Ann, "Crime Scene Soil Samples Get Close Scrutiny from Museum Scientists," Smithsonian Institution.

Internet sites for general soil information:

http://school.discovery.com/schooladventures/soil
Grades 5-8, but nice exercise and description of soil with definitions

http://ltpwww.gsfc.nasa.gov/globe
Site exploring all aspects of soil, elementary level, but useful information

http://soils.ag.uidaho.edu/soilorders
Soil taxonomy information

http://soils.usda.gov/classification/keys/
RevKeysSoilTax8_02.pdf
Everything you ever wanted to know about soil classification in 328 pages!

http://soils.usda.gov/education/facts/
main.htm
Good, simple explanation on soil classification, origin, etc.

Loynachan, Thomas E., Kirk W. Brown, Terence H. Cooper, Murray H. Milford, *Sustaining Our Soils and Society*. American Geological Institute, www.agiweb.org/pubs. General information on soils.

Lynn, Warren C. and Michael J. Pearson, "The Color of Soil," *The Science Teacher* May 2000, 20.

McPhee, John, "The Gravel Page," *New Yorker,* January 29, 1996. Cases and detailed geological descriptions. This material is included in McPhee's, *Irons in the Fire,* Farrar, Straus and Giroux. 1997.

Murray, Raymond, "Devil in the Details, The Science of Forensic Geology," *Geotimes,* February 2000, 14. Cases.

Murray, Raymond C. and John C. F. Tedrow, *Forensic Geology,* Simon & Schuster, (1998). Updated and revised from 1975 book. See also Ray Murray's web site www.forensicgeology.net/science.htm

Murray, Raymond C. and John C. F. Tedrow, *Forensic Science, Earth Sciences and Criminal Investigations,* Rutgers University Press, (1975). This and the above are both out of print.

General References

Evans, Colin, *The Casebook of Forensic Detection.* New York: John Wiley, 1966. Summaries of 100 famous cases solved by forensic science.

Fisher, David, *Hard Evidence.* New York: Dell, 1995. Scientific crime detection in the FBI laboratories with many actual cases and how they were solved.

Kurland, Michael, *How to Solve a Murder.* New York: MacMillon, 1995. Uses a crime scenario to discuss forensic techniques.

Ragle, Larry, *Crime Scene.* New York: Avon Books, 1995. Investigation of crime scenes using actual cases.

Saferstein, Richard, *Criminalistics: An Introduction to Forensic Science, 6th edition.* Upper Saddle River, NJ: Prentice-Hall, 1998. Excellent standard college-level reference for teaching forensic science.

Thorwald, Jürgen, *Crime and Science: The New Frontier in Criminology.* Harcourt, Brace & World: New York 1966. Historical accounts of crimes solved by all types of forensic evidence.

Walker, Pam and Elain Wood, *Crime Scene Investigations.* West Nyack, NY: The Center for Applied research in Education, 1998. Many forensic labs for grades 6–12.

Scientific Supply Companies

Carolina Biological Supply Company
2700 York Road
Burlington, NC 27215
800-334-5551
www.carolina.com

Flinn Scientific, Inc.
P.O. Box 219
Batavia, IL 60510
800-452-1261 Fax: 866-452-1436
www.flinnsci.com

Frey Scientific
P.O. Box 8101
100 Paragon Parkway
Mansfield, OH 44903
800-225-FREY Fax: 877-256-FREY
https://www.freyscientific.com/about_frey.jsp

Sargent-Welch Scientific Co.
P.O. Box 5229
Buffalo Grove, IL 60089-5229
800-727-4368 Fax: 800-676-2540
www.sargentwelch.com

Science Kit and Boreal Laboratories
777 E. Park Drive
PO Box 5003
Tonawanda, NY 14150
800-828-7777 Fax: 800-828-3299
www.sciencekit.com

WARD's Natural Science
P.O. Box 92912
Rochester, NY 14692-9012
800-962-2660
www.wardsci.com/

Fisher Science Education
4500 Turnberry Drive
Hanover Park, IL 60133
800-955-1177
www.fisheredu.com

Educational Innovations
362 Main Avenue
Norwalk, CT 06851
888-912-7474
www.teachersource.com

Arbor Scientific
P.O. Box 2750
Ann Arbor, MI 48106
800-367-6695
www.arborsci.com

Schoolmasters Science
745 State Circle
P.O. Box 1941
Ann Arbor, MI 48106
800-521-2832
www.schoolmasters.com

Forestry Suppliers, Inc.
205 West Rankin Street
P.O. Box 8397
Jackson, MS 39284-8397
800-647-5368
www.forestry-suppliers.com

Sigma-Aldrich Corp.
St. Louis, MO
800-325-3010
www.sigmaaldrich.com

Time Line of Forensic Science

Forensic science, as with all sciences and technology, grew in investigative breadth and depth due to discoveries in the biological, physical, and medical sciences and the development of analytical instrumentation. For example, the microscope allowed advancement in forensic pathology and trace evidence analysis; the camera allowed advances in criminal identification, ballistics, documentation examination. So how did it begin?

66 C.E.—Nero murdered his wife and presented her head on a dish to his mistress. She identified the head as Nero's wife by a black tooth located in the anterior position. Was this the beginning of forensic odontology?

1248—Chinese book described how to distinguish drowning from strangulation.

1514—The earliest reference to blood-spatter evidence was a trial in London in which the victim, Richard Hunne, was jailed on five charges of heresy. One morning Hunne was found hanged in his jail cell. After his death, thirteen additional charges of heresy were brought against Hunne, including one charge for self-murder. After review of both the blood stain and medical evidence the court found, "Whereby it appeareth plainly to us all, that the neck of Hunne was broken, and the great Plenty of Blood was shed before he was hang'd. Wherefore all we find by God and all our Consciences, that Richard Hunne was murdered. Also we acquit the Said Richard Hunne of his own death."

1598—Fortunatus Fidelus was the first to practice forensic medicine in Italy.

1784—First documented case of physical matching when an Englishman was convicted of murder based on a torn edge of a wad of newspaper in a pistol matching a piece remaining in his pocket

1810—First detective force established in Paris, the Sûrcté

1813—Mathiew Orfila, considered the father of modern toxicology, published the first scientific book on poisons—their detection and effects. Poisoning was a popular way of dispatching people. The punishment of a poisoner by Henry III was boiling to death.

1835—First bullet comparison to catch a murderer by Scotland Yard

1836—James Marsh used toxicology in an arsenic poisoning trial.

1849—First dental evidence accepted in a U.S. court in the murder of Dr. George Parkman

1863—First presumptive test for blood using the fact that hemoglobin oxidizes hydrogen peroxide

1880—Scotsman Henry Faulds used fingerprints to eliminate an innocent suspect, similar to instances today using DNA.

1887—Arthur Conan Doyle published his first Sherlock Holmes story.

1892—Francis Galton published his book on fingerprints and their use in solving crimes.

1896—Edward Henry developed the prototype fingerprint classification system now in use Europe and the United States.

1900—Karl Landsteiner discovered human blood groups, leading to blood typing.

1901—Paul Uhlenhuth developed the precipiten test, which was used in the murder conviction of Ludwig Tessnow in the same year.

1904—Edmond Locard formulated his famous principle, "Every contact leaves a trace."

1905—President Theodore Roosevelt established the Federal Bureau of Investigation (FBI).

1910—Victor Balthazard published the first comprehensive study of human and animal hair.

1920s—Georg Popp used botanical and soil identification in solving a crime.

1923—In *Frye v. United States,* polygraph test results were ruled inadmissible, which induced the concept of general acceptance.

1932—The FBI Crime Laboratory was created.

1940—Landsteiner described Rh blood groups.

1950—The American Academy of Forensic Science was formed.

1975—The *Federal Rules of Evidence* were enacted.

1977—The FBI started its computerized Automated Fingerprint Identification System (AFIS).

1986—DNA profiling was used to identify Colin Pitchfork as the murderer of two girls in England.

1991—The Computerized Integrated Ballistics Identification System was developed.

1993—In *Daubert v. Merrell Dow,* the court altered the standard of admission of scientific evidence.

1998—The FBI put a DNA database on-line (NIDIS).

Overheads, Labels, and Forms

EVIDENCE	**EVIDENCE**
Case No. _____	Case No. _____
Date _____	Date _____

EVIDENCE	**EVIDENCE**
Case No. _____	Case No. _____
Date _____	Date _____

EVIDENCE	**EVIDENCE**
Case No. _____	Case No. _____
Date _____	Date _____

EVIDENCE	**EVIDENCE**
Case No. _____	Case No. _____
Date _____	Date _____

EVIDENCE	**EVIDENCE**
Case No. _____	Case No. _____
Date _____	Date _____

EVIDENCE	**EVIDENCE**
Case No. _____	Case No. _____
Date _____	Date _____

Hair Characteristics Chart

Characteristic	Yours	Everyone
1. Color White Blonde Brown Black Red No color—bald		
2. Length (cm) Under 3 cm 3–8 cm 8–15 cm 15–30 cm 30–50 cm over 50 cm		
3. Medulla Absent Fragmentary Interrupted Continuous		
4. Diameter 20–40 μm 40–60 μm 60–80 μm 80–100 μm 100–120 μm		
5. Configuration Straight Curly Kinky		
6. Tip Cut Split Frayed Rounded Pointed		
7. Cosmetic Treatment None Bleached Dyed Other		

EVIDENCE

Description _____

Removed from _____

Address _____

Time _____ Date _____

Received by _____

Time _____ Date _____

EVIDENCE

Description _____

Removed from _____

Address _____

Time _____ Date _____

Received by _____

Time _____ Date _____

EVIDENCE

Description _____

Removed from _____

Address _____

Time _____ Date _____

Received by _____

Time _____ Date _____

EVIDENCE

Description _____

Removed from _____

Address _____

Time _____ Date _____

Received by _____

Time _____ Date _____

133

EVIDENCE

Case No.   Date

Description of Contents:

Chain of Custody

Received From	By	Date	Time

EVIDENCE

Case No.   Date

Description of Contents:

Chain of Custody

Received From	By	Date	Time

Sine Table

Angle	0	0.1	0.2	0.3	0.4	0.5	0.6	0.7	0.8	0.9
0°	.0000	.0017	.0035	.0052	.0070	.0087	.0105	.0122	.0140	.0157
1	.0175	.0192	.0209	.0227	.0244	.0262	.0279	.0297	.0314	.0032
2	.0349	.0366	.0384	.0401	.0419	.0436	.0454	.0471	.0488	.0506
3	.0523	.0541	.0558	.0576	.0593	.0610	.0628	.0645	.0663	.0680
4	.0698	.0715	.0732	.0750	.0767	.0785	.0802	.0819	.0837	.0854
5	.0872	.0889	.0906	.0924	.0941	.0958	.0976	.0993	.1001	.1028
6	.1045	.1063	.1080	.1097	.1115	.1132	.1149	.1167	.1186	.1201
7	.1219	.1236	.1253	.1271	.1288	.1305	.1323	.1340	.1357	.1374
8	.1392	.1409	.1426	.1444	.1461	.1478	.1495	.1513	.1530	.1547
9	.1564	.1582	.1599	.1616	.1633	.1650	.1668	.1685	.1702	.1719
10°	.1736	.1765	.1771	.1788	.1805	.1822	.1840	.1857	.1874	.1891
11	.1908	.1925	.1942	.1959	.1977	.1994	.2011	.2028	.2056	.2062
12	.2079	.2096	.2113	.2130	.2147	.2164	.2181	.2198	.2215	.2233
13	.2250	.2267	.2284	.2300	.2317	.2334	.2351	.2368	.2385	.2402
14	.2419	.2436	.2453	.2470	.2487	.2504	.2521	.2538	.2554	.2571
15	.2588	.2605	.2622	.2639	.2656	.2672	.2689	.2706	.2723	.2740
16	.2756	.2773	.2790	.2807	.2823	.2840	.2857	.2874	.2890	.2907
17	.2924	.2940	.2957	.2974	.2990	.3007	.3024	.3040	.3057	.3074
18	.3090	.3107	.3123	.3140	.3156	.3173	.3190	.3206	.3223	.3239
19	.3256	.3272	.3289	.3305	.3322	.3338	.3355	.3371	.3387	.3404
20°	.3420	.3437	.3453	.3469	.3486	.3502	.3518	.3535	.3551	.3567
21	.3584	.3600	.3616	.3633	.3649	.3665	.3681	.3698	.3714	.3730
22	.3746	.3762	.3778	.3795	.3811	.3827	.3843	.3859	.3875	.3891
23	.3907	.3923	.3939	.3955	.3971	.3987	.4003	.4019	.4035	.4051
24	.4067	.4083	.4099	.4115	.4131	.4147	.4163	.4179	.4195	.4210
25	.4226	.4242	.4258	.4274	.4289	.4305	.4321	.437	.4352	.4368
26	.4384	.4399	.4415	.4431	.4446	.4462	.4478	.4493	.4509	.4524
27	.4540	.4555	.4571	.4586	.4602	.4617	.4633	.4648	.4664	.4679
28	.4695	.4710	.4726	.4741	.4756	.4772	.4787	.4802	.4818	.4833
29	.4848	.4863	.4879	.4894	.4909	.4924	.4939	.4955	.4970	.4985
30°	.5000	.5015	.5035	.5045	.5060	.5075	.5090	.5105	.5120	.5135
31	.5150	.5165	.5180	.5195	.5210	.5225	.5240	.5255	.5270	.5284
32	.5299	.5314	.5329	.5344	.5358	.5373	.5388	.5402	.5417	.5432
33	.5446	.5461	.5476	.5490	.5505	.5519	.5534	.5548	.5563	.5577
34	.5592	.5606	.5621	.5635	.5650	.5664	.5678	.5693	.5707	.5721
35	.5736	.5750	.5764	.5779	.5793	.5807	.5821	.5835	.5850	.5864
36	.5878	.5892	.5906	.5920	.5934	.5948	.5962	.5976	.5990	.6004
37	.6018	.6032	.6046	.6060	.6074	.6088	.6101	.6115	.6129	.6143
38	.6157	.6170	.6184	.6198	.6211	.6225	.6239	.6252	.6266	.6280
39	.6293	.6307	.6320	.6334	.6347	.6361	.6374	.6388	.6401	.6414
40°	.6428	.6441	.6455	.6468	.6481	.6494	.6508	.6521	.6534	.6547
41	.6561	.6574	.6587	.6600	.6613	.6626	.6639	.6652	.6665	.6678
42	.6691	.6704	.6717	.6730	.6743	.6756	.6769	.6782	.6794	.6807
43	.6820	.6833	.6845	.6858	.6871	.6884	.6896	.6909	.6921	.6934
44	.6947	.6959	.6972	.6984	.6997	.7009	.7022	.7034	.7046	.7059

(continued)

Sine Table *(continued)*

Angle	0	0.1	0.2	0.3	0.4	0.5	0.6	0.7	0.8	0.9
45°	.7071	.7283	.8096	.7108	.7120	.7133	.7145	.7157	.7169	.7181
46	.7193	.7206	.7218	.7230	.7242	.7254	.7266	.7278	.7290	.7302
47	.7314	.7325	.7337	.7349	.7361	.7373	.7385	.7396	.7408	.7420
48	.7431	.7443	.7455	.7466	.7478	.7490	.7501	.7513	.7524	.7536
49	.7547	.7559	.7570	.7581	.7593	.7604	.7615	.7627	.7638	.7649
50°	.7660	.7672	.7683	.7694	.7705	.7716	.7727	.7738	.7749	.7760
51	.7771	.7782	.7793	.7804	.7815	.7826	.7837	.7848	.7859	.7869
52	.7880	.7891	.7902	.7912	.7921	.7934	.7944	.7955	.7965	.7976
53	.7986	.7997	.8007	.8018	.8028	.8039	.8059	.8059	.8070	.8080
54	.8090	.8100	.8111	.8121	.8131	.8141	.8151	.8161	.8171	.8181
55	.8192	.8202	.8211	.8221	.8231	.8241	.8251	.8261	.8371	.8281
56	.8290	.8300	.8310	.8320	.8329	.8339	.8348	.8358	.8368	.8377
57	.8387	.8396	.8406	.8415	.8425	.8434	.8443	.8453	.8462	.8471
58	.8480	.8490	.8499	.8508	.8517	.8526	.8536	.8545	.8554	.8563
59	.8572	.8581	.8590	.8599	.8607	.8616	.8625	.8634	.8643	.8652
60°	.8660	.8669	.8678	.8686	.8695	.8704	.8712	.8721	.8729	.8738
61	.8746	.8755	.8763	.8771	.8780	.8788	.8796	.8805	.8813	.8821
62	.8829	.8838	.8846	.8854	.8862	.8870	.8878	.8886	.8894	.8902
63	.8910	.8918	.8926	.8934	.8942	.8949	.8957	.8965	.8973	.8980
64	.8988	.8996	.9003	.9011	.9018	.9026	.9033	.9041	.9048	.9056
65	.9063	.9070	.9078	.9085	.9092	.9100	.9107	.9114	.9121	.9128
66	.9135	.9143	.9150	.9157	.9164	.9171	.9178	.9184	.9191	.9198
67	.9205	.9212	.9219	.9225	.9232	.9239	.9245	.9252	.9259	.9265
68	.9272	.9278	.9285	.9291	.9298	.9304	.9311	.9317	.9323	.9330
69	.9336	.9342	.9348	.9354	.9361	.9367	.9373	.9379	.9385	.9391
70°	.9397	.9403	.9409	.9415	.9421	.9426	.9432	.9438	.9444	.9449
71	.9455	.9461	.9466	.9472	.9478	.9483	.9489	.9494	.9500	.9505
72	.9511	.9516	.9521	.9527	.9532	.9537	.9542	.9548	.9553	.9558
73	.9563	.9568	.9573	.9578	.9583	.9588	.9593	.9598	.9603	.9608
74	.9613	.9617	.9622	.9627	.9632	.9636	.9641	.9646	.9650	.9655
75	.9659	.9664	.9668	.9673	.9677	.9681	.9686	.9690	.9694	.9699
76	.9703	.9707	.9711	.9715	.9720	.9724	.9728	.9732	.9736	.9740
77	.9744	.9748	.9751	.9755	.9759	.9763	.9767	.9770	.9774	.9778
78	.9781	.9785	.9789	.9792	.9796	.9799	.9803	.9806	.9810	.9813
79	.9816	.9820	.9821	.9826	.9829	.9833	.9836	.9839	.9842	.9845
80°	.9848	.9851	.9854	.9857	.9860	.9863	.9866	.9869	.9871	.9874
81	.9877	.9880	.9882	.9885	.9888	.9890	.9893	.9895	.9898	.9900
82	.9903	.9905	.9907	.9910	.9912	.9914	.9917	.9919	.9921	.9923
83	.9925	.9928	.9930	.9932	.9934	.9936	.9938	.9940	.9942	.9943
84	.9945	.9947	.9949	.9951	.9952	.9954	.9956	.9957	.9959	.9960
85	.9962	.9963	.9965	.9966	.9968	.9969	.9970	.9972	.9973	.9974
86	.9976	.9977	.9978	.9979	.9980	.9981	.9982	.9983	.9984	.9985
87	.9986	.9987	.9988	.9989	.9990	.9990	.9991	.9992	.9993	.9993
88	.9994	.9995	.9995	.9996	.9996	.9997	.9997	.9997	.9998	.9998
89	.9998	.9999	.9999	.9999	.9999	1.000	1.000	1.000	1.000	1.000

ABO classification system: blood types based on two antigens labeled A and B

admissible: allowed in court; see Rules of Evidence

agglutination: a reaction that takes place when antigens and antibodies link together, creating clumping together of cells

amino acids: chief components of proteins that are synthesized by cells

amorphous: non-crystalline, or the atoms or units are arranged randomly; this accounts for the fracture pattern and many of the optical properties of glass compared to crystalline material, such as quartz

anagen phase: a phase of hair growth during which the hair root has a pointed end and is attached to the follicle for continued growth

angle of incidence: the angle light makes when traveling into another medium

angle of refraction: the angle light makes when traveling out of one medium and into another

antibodies: produced by white blood cells for the immune system

antigen: a protein found on the surface of red blood cells that characterizes blood type

antiserum: a serum containing antibodies that will react against a particular antigen

bivalent: blood cells that have two antigen sites

blood factors: characteristics used to classify blood type

blowback: glass fragments recoiling backwards toward the direction of impact; also applicable to any violent impact

catagen phase: a stage in hair growth during which the root becomes elongated after the anagen phase and before the telogen phase

chemical property: the behavior of a substance when it reacts with another substance

chemiluminescence: emission of light from a chemical reaction

chromatogram: the record of a chromatographic separation; see chromatography

chromatography: a method of separating components of mixtures based upon preferential adsorption or partitioning of components in a gas, liquid, or solution; in paper chromatography, the cellulose of the paper acts as the adsorbing medium

circumstantial evidence: evidence that implies a fact or event

class evidence: evidence that is found to be consistent with a particular source. It can be associated with a particular group of items that share properties or characteristics

concentric fracture: a crack in glass that roughly forms a circle around the point of impact

conchoidal: a rough, uneven surface

consistent with: meaning there is no difference between the measured properties of the standard or known material and the questioned evidence; if, however, the characteristics of the questioned material are found to be inconsistent with the standard or known material, then it could not have originated from that source.

cortex: inside the cuticle of hair, consisting of keratin molecules

criminalistics: used interchangeably with forensic science as the application of science to the analysis of crime scenes and crimes

cuticle: the outer covering of the hair shaft

Daubert ruling: rule of evidence stating that the trial judge must assume responsibility for admissibility and validity based on guidelines given by the U.S. Supreme Court

density: a physical property of a material that is its mass per unit volume

direct evidence: evidence based on a person's five senses

elute: to extract one material from another, usually by means of a solvent

entomology: the study of insects

erythrocytes: red blood cells that contain hemoglobin and transport oxygen and carbon dioxide

false-positive: a test result that comes out positive when it is not. Usually caused by contamination or lack of running a control

felony: a major crime such as a violent crime, computer fraud, auto theft, forgery, or the sale of illegal drugs

fiber: composed of many filaments twisted or bonded together to form a thread or yarn

filament: a single strand of material, usually twisted with other filaments to make a thread or fiber

flotation method: based on the idea that a particle will float on a liquid that is more dense than the particle, sink in a liquid that is less dense than the particle, and remain suspended in a liquid of equal density

fluorescence: a property of a material that absorbs light of a shorter wavelength and emits light of a longer wavelength

forensic science: the study and application of science to matters of the law

Frye standard: rule of evidence that states that scientific evidence must be given by an expert witness and have gained "general acceptance" in the relevant field of study

hair follicle: a bulb-shaped pocket in the skin that hair grows out of

hemoglobin: an oxygen carrier in red blood cells

Hematest™ and Hemastix™: commercial tests to determine the presence of blood

histogram: a chart showing a representation of a frequency distribution

ICP spectrometry: inductively coupled plasma spectroscopy used for elemental analysis

independent events: two or more events, observations, or actions that are not related to one another

indirect evidence: evidence that does not prove a fact

individualized evidence: evidence that can be traced back to a single source

ion: an atom or molecule that has lost or gained one or more electrons and thus has a net positive or negative charge

Kastle-Meyer: a color test to determine the presence of blood

keratin: fibrous protein that forms the chemical base for hair

lachrymator: a tear-producing substance

leukocytes: white blood cells that produce antibodies used in the immune system

Locard's principle: the theory that whenever two objects are in contact, there is an exchange or transfer of material

luminol test: a chemiluminescence test to determine the presence of blood

material: evidence that addresses the issue of the particular crime

medulla: a row of cells running through the middle of a hair shaft. It can be used to determine whether a particular hair is human or animal

metabolites: organic molecules involved in the process of metabolism, the sum of all chemical processes occurring in an organism; metabolites can either form more complex molecules or result from the degradation of compounds.

Miranda rights: statement read to a person at arrest, informing the individual of his or her Constitutional right against self-incrimination (5th Amendment) and access to counsel (6th Amendment)

misdemeanor: a minor crime; punishment may be up to 12 months in jail or up to $1,000 in fines

mitochondrial DNA: DNA that is found in the mitochondria of cells

neutron activation analysis: method of determining elements by inducing radioactivity in a sample

nuclear DNA: DNA that is found in the nucleus of cells

odontology: the study of teeth and dental records

optical brighteners: colorless dyes that cause blue light to be reflected, thereby creating a whiter object

organic: substances composed primarily of hydrocarbons (carbon and hydrogen); conversely, inorganic substances contain a preponderance of elements other than C and H, such as Si, O, Mg, Al, Fe, Ca, and K in soils

pathology: the study of unexplained or unusual death

peroxides: chemical compounds that have two oxygen atoms bonded together, such as hydrogen peroxide, HOOH or H_2O_2

pH: the acidity of a solution is described by pH, a number that represents the hydrogen ion concentration in a solution: $pH = -\log[H^+]$

physical evidence: any object or material that is relevant in a crime or crime scene

physical property: a characteristic that does not involve a change in the identity of a substance, such as odor, color, density, or refractive index

plasma: the fluid portion of the blood, composed of water and metabolites

platelets: solid portion of blood that initiates the clotting process

polygraphy: the study of lie detection

polymer: a molecule consisting of many repeating units; it can be naturally occurring or synthetic

precipitate: a solid substance that forms from a solution

precipitin test: standard test used to determine if blood origin is human or animal

presumptive test: a preliminary test used to determine whether or not further testing is required

probable cause: evidence that a crime was committed and the accused committed it; for a felony, usually determined in a preliminary hearing

probative: evidence that proves something

qualitative: referring to what kind

radial fracture: a crack in glass that originates from the point of impact and radiates outward

refraction: a change in direction and velocity of light when it passes from one medium into another

refractive index: a physical property of a material that will transmit light. It is the ratio of the velocity of light in a vacuum to the velocity of light in a particular medium

retention factor (RF): in paper or TLC chromatography, RF is equal to the distance from the origin to the spot divided by the distance from the origin to the solvent front

rhesus factor (Rh): a blood factor that distinguishes Rh+ and Rh– blood types

Rule of Large Numbers: the computed probability approaches the actual probability as population increases

Rules of Evidence: rules that govern admissibility of evidence in court; evidence must be significant, relevant, and presented by credible witnesses

secretors: approximately 80% of the population whose blood-type antigens are found in body fluids other than just blood

serology: the study of body fluids using specific antigen and serum antibody reactions

serum: the yellowish liquid that separates from blood when a clot is formed

Snell's law: a ratio of the angle of incidence to the angle of refraction as light travels from one medium to another

spinnerette: nozzle used to form liquid/molten polymers into filaments

sublime: passing from a solid directly to a gas without passing through a liquid state; for example, dry ice, iodine, and moth balls undergo sublimation

supernatant: liquid remaining after particles or precipitate has settled

taxonomy: a system of classification

telogen phase: a phase in hair growth when the hair is in a resting phase and the root takes on a club-like appearance

texture: a property of soil related to particle size

testimonial evidence: a statement made under oath, also called direct evidence

thin layer chromatography (TLC): type of chromatography in which the silica gel or alumina selectively adsorbs the components of the mixture; see chromatography

trilobal: type of cross section of synthetic fiber with three lobes

warp: lengthwise yarn or thread in a weave

weft: crosswise yarn or thread in a weave

yarn: a continuous strand of fibers or filaments, either twisted or not

A

abduction, attempted, 53
ABO classification system, 56–59
   creation of, 56
   importance of, 58
acetic acid, 39
administrative law, 3
admissible evidence, 5
adsorption, 50
agglutination, 58
amino acids, 15
amorphous, 70
anagen phase, 18
angle of incidence, 77
angle of refraction, 77
antibodies, 56, 57
   bivalent nature of, 58
antigens, 56–57, 58
antiserum, 57
arrest, 3
arrest warrant, 3
assault, 63–64

B

bail, 3
blood, 58–59. *See also* Blood Spatter Analysis
   components of, 56–57
   detection of (student lab), 60–61
   as forensic evidence, 56–58
   pattern analysis (student lab), 68
   testing human or animal (student lab), 62
   typing, 56–58
blood factors, 56
Blood Spatter Analysis, 67
blowback, 83
Brannen, Melissa, 31
bromoform, 71, 93
burden of proof, 3
burglary, 80

C

capital punishment, 2
case law, 2
catagen phase, 18
chemical properties, 36
chemiluminescence, 62
chromatogram, 50
chromatography, 50
circumstantial evidence, 5, 23
civil law, 2, 5
class evidence, 6–7, 23
   fiber as, 6, 33
   glass fragments as, 6, 69
   hair as, 6, 23, 33
   soil as, 6
concentric fracture, 83
conchoidal fracture, 69
Congress, 2
Constitution, 2
cortex (of hair shaft), 17
crime
   categories of, 2
   collection of evidence from, 3
crime laboratories, 1
criminalistics, 1
criminal law, 2, 5
cuticle (of hair shaft), 17, 25

D

Daubert ruling, 5, 6
Daubert v. Merrell Dow Pharmaceutical, Inc., 6
decomposition
chemical, 36
thermal, 36, 39
defendant, 3
density, 69
   of glass, 69
   of a glass fragment, measuring (student lab),
      73–74

profile of soil (student lab), 91

and refractive index of fibers, 43

direct evidence, 4

Disch, Eva, 87–88

DNA

analysis, 56

extraction from hair, 15

fingerprinting, 6

dognapping, 27–28

dyes

chromatography of, 50

dyeing different fabrics (student lab), 48–49

E

elution, 51

entomology, 1

equity law, 2

erythrocytes, 56, 57

ethical issues, *viii*

evidence, 3. *See also* forensic evidence

admissible, 5

common physical, 4

crime scene, 3

evaluation of, 1

importance of physical, 5

individual vs. class, 6–7

preponderance of, 2

types of, 4–7

expert witness, 1, 5

F

fabrics, 31

dyeing different (student lab), 48–49

as evidence, 34

three basic weave patterns of, 34

false-positive, 61

FBI, 87

felony, 3

fiber

as class evidence, 33

composition of, 31

cross sections (student lab), 45–46

density and refractive index of, 43

as forensic evidence, 31

identification of, by chemical properties, 36

microscopic examination of (student lab), 33–35

observing fluorescence in (student lab), 47

filament, 31

fingerprints, 6

Fisher, David, 83

flotation method, 73

fluorescence

in fibers, 47

in glass, 69

forensic activity

assault, 63–64

attempted abduction, 53

burglary, 80

dognapping, 27–28

robbery, 11

theft, 96

forensic evidence. *See also* evidence

blood as, 56–59

glass as, 69–70

hair as, 15

importance of fiber as, 31

soil as, 87–88

Forensic Geology (Murray and Tedrow), 88

forensic science

Blood Spatter Analysis, 67

definition of, 1

hair, as class evidence in, 23

importance of blood typing in, 58–59

time line of, 129–130

use of chromatograms in, 50

forensic scientists, 1, 4

finding a common source, and, 43

individualizing evidence and, 6

forensic serology, 56, 58

Frye standard, 5–6

Frye v. United States, 5

G

glass

components of, 69

composition of (chart), 70

density of, 69

as forensic evidence, 69–70

fracture patterns, analysis of (student lab), 86

fracture patterns of, 83–85

fragment, measuring density of (student lab), 73–74

fragments, determining refractive index of (student lab), 78–79

pieces, examination of (student lab), 71–72

refractive index of, 75

H

hair

as class evidence, 6, 23

comparison of animal and human (student lab), 25–26

configuration, 17

diameter, 17

as forensic evidence, 15

microscopic examination of human (student lab), 19–22

morphology of human, 17–18

root, 18

structure, 17

tip, 18

hair follicle, 15

Hard Evidence (Fisher), 83

hearing, 1

non-jury, 3

hearsay, 5

Hemastix test strip, 60

Hematest tablet, 60

hemoglobin, 56, 60

histogram, 78

Hughes, Cal, 31

I

ICP (inductively coupled plasma) spectrometry, 69

independent events, 12–13

indirect evidence, 5

individualized evidence, 6–7

injunction, 2

Internal Revenue Service (IRS), 3

J

jury, 3, 5

K

Kastle-Meyer color test, 61

keratin, 15, 17

Kirks, Dr. Paul, 67

L

lachrymator, 93

Landsteiner, Karl, 56

Laubach, Karl, 88

legal system, 2–3

terms used in, 12

leukocytes, 56, 57

litmus paper, 39

Locard, Edmond, 4

Locard's principle, 4

luminescence, 61

luminol test, 61

M

medulla (of hair shaft), 17, 25

medullary index (MI), 25

metabolites, 56

Miranda rights, 3

misdemeanor, 2, 3

mitochondrial DNA, 15

Munsell Soil Color Charts, The, 90

Murray, Raymond C., 88

N

National Science Education Standards, *vii*
neutron activation analysis, 69
nuclear DNA, 15

O

odontology, 1
optical brighteners, 47
organic, 93
oxidation, 36

P

pathology, 1
peers, 3
peroxides, 61
pH, 94
physical evidence, 4
physical properties, 36
plaintiff, 2
plasma, 56
platelets, 56
plea, 3
polygraphy, 1
polymers, 15, 36. *See also* fiber
    chemical composition of, 41
Popp, Georg, 88
precedents, 2
precipitin test, 62
presumptive tests, 60
probability, 5, 12–13, 23–24
probable cause, 3, 12
prosecutor, 3
public law, 2

Q

qualitative, 95

R

radial fracture, 83
reasonable doubt, 2, 12

red blood cells. *See* erythrocytes
refraction, 75
refractive index, 75
    determining (student lab), 76–77
    of fibers, 43
    of glass, 69
    of glass fragments, determining (student lab),
        78–79
restraining order, 2
retention factor (RF), 52
rhesus factor (Rh), 56, 58
Rh factor, 56, 58
robbery, 11
rubrics
    assessing crime reports, 122
    assessing essays, 123
    assessing laboratory reports, 121
Rule of Large Numbers, 12
Rules of Evidence, 5

S

safety, *viii*
scientific method, *vi*
secretors, 56
serology, 56, 58
serum, 56
    antibodies in, 57
Sheppard, Marilyn, 67
Sheppard, Sam, 67
silica, 69
sine table, 135–136
Snell's law, 76
Social Security Administration, 3
soil
    chemical properties of (student lab), 94–95
    definition of, 87
    density profile of (student lab), 93
    examination of (student lab), 89
    as forensic evidence, 87–88
    physical properties of (student lab), 90–91
    texture of (student lab), 92

speed of light, 75

spinnerette, 45

stare decisis, 2

statement under oath, 4

statistics, 5, 12–13, 23

statutory law, 2

stress marks, 84

student labs

    analysis of glass fracture patterns, 86

    blood pattern analysis, 68

    burning tests, 37–38

    chemical properties of soil (student lab), 94–95

    chemical tests, 41–42

    chromatography of dyes, 50–52

    comparison of animal and human hair, 25–26

    density profile of soil, 93

    detection of blood, 61–62

    determining refractive index, 76–77

    determining refractive index of glass fragments, 78–79

    dyeing different fabrics, 48–49

    examination of fiber cross sections, 45–46

    examination of glass pieces, 71–72

    examination of soil, 89

    measuring the density of a glass fragment, 73–74

    microscopic examination of fibers, 33–35

    microscopic examination of human hair, 19–22

    observing fluorescence in fibers, 47

    physical properties of soil, 90–91

    testing human or animal blood, 63

    texture of soil, 92

    thermal decomposition, 39–40

sublimation, 52

supernatant, 95

suspect, 3

    characteristics or objects linking, 23

T

taxonomy, 69

Tedrow, John C. F., 88

telogen phase, 18

testimonial evidence, 4

texture, 92

theft, 96

thin-layer chromatography (TLC), 50

trajectory, 86

trial, 1, 3

U

ultraviolet (UV) radiation, 47

U.S. criminal justice system, 2–3

U.S. Supreme Court, 67

V

voiceprints, 6

W

warp, 34

weave, 34

weft, 34

white blood cells. *See* leukocytes

witnesses, 3, 4

X

xylene, 93

Y

yarn, 34

Share Your Bright Ideas with Us!

We want to hear from you! Your valuable comments and suggestions will help us meet your current and future classroom needs.

Your name_____Date_____

School name_____

School address_____

City _____State _____Zip_____Phone number (_____)_____

Grade level taught_____Subject area(s) taught_____Average class size_____

Where did you purchase this publication?_____

Was your salesperson knowledgeable about this product?   Yes_____   No_____

What monies were used to purchase this product?

___School supplemental budget   ___Federal/state funding   ___Personal

Please "grade" this Walch publication according to the following criteria:

	A	B	C	D	F
Quality of service you received when purchasing	A	B	C	D	F
Ease of use	A	B	C	D	F
Quality of content	A	B	C	D	F
Page layout	A	B	C	D	F
Organization of material	A	B	C	D	F
Suitability for grade level	A	B	C	D	F
Instructional value	A	B	C	D	F

COMMENTS:_____

_____

What specific supplemental materials would help you meet your current—or future—instructional needs?

_____

Have you used other Walch publications? If so, which ones?_____

May we use your comments in upcoming communications?   ___Yes   ___No

Please **FAX** this completed form to **207-772-3105**, or mail it to:

Product Development, J. Weston Walch, Publisher, P. O. Box 658, Portland, ME 04104-0658

We will send you a **FREE GIFT** as our way of thanking you for your feedback. **THANK YOU!**